Th
Pleiadian House
of Initiation

"A great, creative achievement; excellent writing and observation of a life lived with awakened awareness, this seeming make-believe world is absolutely real. *The Pleiadian House of Initiation* is a brilliant tapestry of vision, culture, religions, and nature. Like Grandmother Spider, Mary Beben has spun her web and flung it into the sky, reminding us we come from the stars. This book is her healing initiation. It is both her Psalmistry and her Song of Songs."

RISA D'ANGELES, WRITER, TEACHER, AND FOUNDER AND
DIRECTOR OF THE ESOTERIC AND ASTROLOGICAL STUDIES AND
RESEARCH AND HEALING INSTITUTE

"Beben's holographic prose transports the reader into a multidimensional yet intimate experience of accessing the higher realms that reside within us. *The Pleiadian House of Initiation* is a wonderful and uplifting guide. A real treasure during this time of conscious evolution."

DANIELLE RAMA HOFFMAN, AUTHOR OF
THE COUNCIL OF LIGHT AND *THE TEMPLES OF LIGHT*

"Examining her house of many rooms—a classic metaphor for the soul—illuminated by profound images and wisdom derived from decades of dream and meditation, Mary Beben offers us a great treasure: her soul's odyssey."

MARGARET STARBIRD, AUTHOR OF
THE WOMAN WITH THE ALABASTER JAR

"If you have not yet discovered the magical and visionary work of Mary T. Beben, now is the time. This book will appeal to lovers of the Pleiadian Mystery schools everywhere."

ANAIYA SOPHIA, AUTHOR OF
SACRED SEXUAL UNION AND COAUTHOR OF WOMB WISDOM

"Mary Beben's *The Pleiadian House of Initiation* invites the reader to accompany her on an extraordinary journey to the Oneness of the galaxies. Informed by years of prayer, reflection, and study, Beben finds the words to relate her amazing visionary quest and to approach the ineffable. The reader is rewarded with rare insight into the ongoing evolution of the universe and our role as co-creators with the Holy One. The author's graceful prose flows from image to image, reflecting the dreamlike quality of her journey. Mary Beben challenges us to unlock the love fibers encoded in our DNA."

SUSAN TIBERGHIEN, AUTHOR OF
ONE YEAR TO A WRITING LIFE,
LOOKING FOR GOLD, AND CIRCLING TO THE CENTER

The
Pleiadian House
of Initiation

A Journey through the Rooms
of the Wisdomkeepers

Mary T. Beben

Bear & Company
Rochester, Vermont • Toronto, Canada

Bear & Company
One Park Street
Rochester, Vermont 05767
www.BearandCompanyBooks.com

Bear & Company is a division of Inner Traditions International

Library of Congress Cataloging-in-Publication Data

Beben, Mary T., 1936–

The Pleiadian House of initiation : a journey through the rooms of the wisdomkeepers / Mary T. Beben.

 pages cm

Summary: "A step-by-step tour through our spiritual home in the Pleiades" — Provided by publisher.

ISBN 978-1-59143-191-6 (pbk.) — ISBN 978-1-59143-773-4 (e-book)

1. Spirituality—Miscellanea. 2. Pleiades—Miscellanea. I. Title.

BF1999.B3875 2014

130—dc23

2014005297

Printed and bound in the United States by Versa Press, Inc.

10 9 8 7 6 5 4 3 2 1

Text design and layout by Debbie Glogover
This book was typeset in Garamond Premier Pro with ITC Goudy Sans Std and Gill Sans MT Pro as display fonts

To send correspondence to the author of this book, mail a first-class letter to the author c/o Inner Traditions • Bear & Company, One Park Street, Rochester, VT 05767, and we will forward the communication, or contact the author directly at the Institute for Biodynamic Spirituality at **www.biodynamicspirituality.com**.

This book is lovingly dedicated to the generation
of lovers who will renew the planet,
watering the desert places
and fashioning their swords into pruning hooks.
Love and gratitude be to the Keepers of Earth
—past, present, and future—
and to the bards who have told her true story
through their songs and memories.

Contents

Foreword

By Barbara Hand Clow

Mary Beben's *Pleiadian House of Initiation* invites all of us to inhabit our home in the subtle realms. Like a child who is beckoned through the doorway into the land of make believe, this wonderful book entices us to enter the mansion in the stars—a home with many levels, rooms, and inhabitants. We find hidden places containing forgotten fairy tales and treasured myths from long ago—childhood innocence that has matured to adult wisdom.

Why is the Pleiades our home in the stars? Mary Beben suggests it is because the Pleiades is a home to which we can ascend in consciousness while being rooted in Earth. My own connection with the Pleiades has always been my source of *deep memory*. When I was young, my grandparents, who were my teachers, told me I came from the Pleiades. As an adult, I was delighted to discover that humans have reported connections with the Pleiades for more than 40,000 years, even 100,000 years. I think the modern discovery of ancient connections with the Pleiades is part of the return of the goddess culture. For example, Athena of Greece and Neith of Egypt were goddesses from the Pleiades. Even the Bible refers to the Pleiades as a spiritual home.

Beben says she uses "the Pleiades" as a metaphor for a higher plane at which we experience the unity of all beings in the Divine. We seem to need a home in the higher planes, just as we need one here on Earth. For Christians, the Catholic mysteries have long been profound metaphors for very high states of consciousness. Yet recent confusion in the Roman Catholic Church has caused many people to lose their sense of connection with these mystical states. Beben's book redeems some of these mysteries in light of modern consciousness, which opens our minds and hearts. When our hearts open, they fill with clarity and compassion. Then we remember our spiritual home—the Pleiades—a place for reflection, meditation, and contemplation. She describes a deep flow of activity that pulses through the entire house in the Pleiades, which feels like the heart of the cosmos. She says that in this house dreams filter down to us as sleeping initiates, and we awaken. There is much deep wisdom in this book, as well as a very moving human dimension.

The Pleiadian House of Initiation is honest about our human limitations, which Beben delves into by briefly sharing her own life. As a woman approaching age eighty who was suddenly abandoned about ten years ago by her husband, just before the celebration of their fiftieth wedding anniversary, Beben plunged into the dark night of the soul. In the throes of a life-changing spiritual journey, she became one with the suffering of all. Yet she also found that the veils of separation to other worlds melted away as she suffered. Her story of being escorted to hell to view every possible scene of human cruelty and abuse is unforgettable. As it was happening, she knew that everything she saw was actually happening in the moment; her journey into hell was real, not a dream, and it freed her. She left behind past history and all former life, and found the "eternal now."

In my own experience, mysteriously in resonance with the author's, the eternal now *is* the Pleiades, a timeless world that is home for the human heart. Lately many people have told me they feel a connection with the Pleiades. They seem to be living fully on Earth while experiencing the pinnacle of human evolution. As Beben says, we are realizing we are spiritual beings who descended to Earth to experience biological life. We are to bring this experience back to the Pleiades, back into the higher planes. It is another way of saying something I said in *The Pleiadian Agenda* twenty years ago: "At the pinnacle of human evolution, our species will seed the universe." We are getting ready to send ourselves out into the cosmos, and the appearance of Mary Beben's book reminds us we have attained our evolutionary climb through 100,000 years of human consciousness to seek spirit. *The Pleiadian House of Initiation* is one of the keys to the door into higher dimensions; there our arrival is awaited with joyful anticipation.

BARBARA HAND CLOW is an internationally acclaimed ceremonial teacher, author, and Mayan Calendar researcher. Her numerous books include *The Pleiadian Agenda, Alchemy of Nine Dimensions, Awakening the Planetary Mind, Astrology and the Rising of Kundalini,* and *The Mayan Code.* She has taught at sacred sites throughout the world and maintains an astrological web site, www.HandClow2012.com.

Acknowledgments

Gratitude and honor are due to so many beings and people, some seen and some unseen. Countless teachers, mentors, writers, healers, and encouragers of all sorts must remain unnamed. But there are a few shining souls who have led the way and made this work possible in so special a way that I must extend my humble and best thanks to them.

The Prayer Community of Emmanuel, especially Sue Gehringer, who has borne this work with me as a sister for forty years.

Dr. Bonnie Damron, whose guidance and wisdom made all the difference.

Barbara Hand Clow, who met me on the path and gave me shelter.

Ginny Koenig and Terry Holman, who believed in the work and spent hours helping me sort my thoughts and many drafts.

Susan Tiberghien, whose wise book *One Year to a Writing Life* encouraged and fostered my writing in new ways.

It goes without saying that the largest debt of gratitude goes to the Source from whom all blessings flow, and to those who sculpt and work and dream into flesh the Divine Vision.

PREFACE

Invitation to Ascension

We are a family of beings who recognize the great cosmos as our home. Delighted to call ourselves a smaller, more intimate family, we are also citizens of Earth, the planet we love best. It is my deepest desire that those who enter into these pages will find new joy in belonging to the frail and strong, lowly and royal race of earthlings. We have come through eons of transformation in order to join the alliance of all beings who share our amazing cosmic home. As we pursue our task of rebuilding our home planet, we are assured of deep love and filial support from other beings who inhabit all the dimensions. In love there is no separation; in love we are one.

You are invited to embark on an allegorical tour along a spiritual path, as a person living on Earth in the twenty-first century experiences it. The adventures you will read about are absolutely true, but these things cannot be expressed in the language of our everyday speech. Therefore they are woven of a less dense, more subtle fabric that might touch your heart, rather than bombard your senses. There is also a glimpse here of the future of life on Earth. It points the way to "ascension" as an opening to higher realms of existence that are natural to our human experience.

My greatest concern is that this call to a deeper spirituality might be misunderstood as an escape from the world we share with all other beings on the planet. Nothing could be further from the truth. This is a prophetic vision of our evolution—of all and each of us—into a more grounded and fulfilling destiny right here on this amazing orb we call our home.

It is a call to fully enter into our Earth-based reality as the key to evolution and bliss, as we build our home here. The Pleiades star cluster, also known in astronomy as the Seven Sisters, is used on this journey as a metaphor for a higher plane from which we can experience the unity of all beings in the Divine.* Instead of thinking of Pleiadian beings as extraterrestrials, we are being asked to entertain the likelihood that "they" are ascended facets of "us," reaching out to us from our own higher knowing and opening our hearts beyond limitations imposed by a belief system of separateness. This work encourages the necessary opening of the heart to allow us to access higher consciousness, clarity, and compassion. Ascension will not mean departing Earth, but rather rising to a new platform that will allow us to see our many problems from a perspective beyond the conflicts of warring opposites. This has been called the fifth dimension—a place beyond the tunnel vision of the

---

*The Pleiades star cluster, comprised of extremely luminous stars that have formed within the last 100 million years, is among the nearest star clusters to Earth and is the one most visible in the night sky. In some cultures our sun is seen to be the eighth star in this cluster, closely associated with the Pleiades.

third and fourth dimensions.* It is not a promise of paradisia-
cal bliss but an assurance that we will see and feel the answers
that appear when hearts are transformed and joy rediscovered.

Our personal mythologies enlighten our way and lead us
into adventures of joy, sorrow, and, ultimately, transformation.
I share some of mine here in order to encourage you to keep on
the path you recognize for yourself.

In this book I speak of God, or the Divine, as consubstan-
tial with Love, wherein we all live and have life. I also speak of
other places in the universe, such as the Pleiades, as places we
can be equally at home. I speak of these places metaphorically,
for at no time do we ever abandon our jewel of a planet. The
higher we ascend in consciousness, the more we are grounded
and rooted in the place of our physical embodiment. Non-
earthly spiritual beings cannot fully exist in their own dimensions unless we partner with them here on Earth. We cannot
exist in all of our full potential unless we partner with these
higher energies, intelligences, and inspirations that are not
bound by physical form.

I invite you to join me in visiting some of these other realms
that enhance and support our own. We are the keepers of the
planet that is celebrated in song and story throughout the universe. Please join in the celebration. May you be lifted on wings
of love as you share this testimony.

---

*The dimension above material form that is reachable through ascension beyond
dualities. It is a state we can attain as we rise above "taking sides" and getting
trapped in the gravitational pull of the opposites. It is the realm of love and
light.

TALIESIN'S HARP

Across the centuries our music
rings,
down the
      eddies of time
           it swirls,
curling itself
      like mist
   to fit through keyholes
          and wormholes,
finding one another with
      our song. Who else
could we be yearning for,
             my bard?
We splash
      in little pools of time,
watching the Great Song
          emerge
          from timeless sea,
invisible,
  hovering on horizon,
        flashing now and then
          like heat lightning
    while we try to weave
        the sound, the call,
          the pleading, yearning ache
of Earth's enormous heart
        into melody,
send it
   to lonely stars who tremble
        at her voice.

MARY T. BEBEN

Taliesen was a legendary British court poet whose sixth-century work is believed
to have survived as part of a Middle Welsh manuscript, the *Book of Taliesin*. He is
reputed to have sung at the courts of at least three Celtic British kings.

ONE

Little House in the Pleiades

This house I thought I had discovered is one that has been in my family for centuries, or eons. I am just now rediscovering my home in the Pleiades after having been away for a very long time. It is good to reconnect with my former and eternal life. I will try to relate what takes place here.

The house seems to be empty at first entrance, but is it? To explore it with me, you will first have to understand the rules of Pleiadian existence. If it seems strange at first, just follow. I am sure you, too, will begin to remember as you walk with me. Then it will seem like the most natural thing ever.

The most pervasive feeling of this place right now is the amazing capacity of the mansion. I begin to feel ashamed that I have not occupied it for such a long time, but then I recall there was a reason for that. The house is no worse off for my absence; nothing has deteriorated. It holds all the potential that it ever had.

From the outside it appears to be built of solid brick and has three levels. But observing carefully from a side view, I see there are really four. This is only part of the mystery of this

1

place. The furnishings are well preserved; the walls, floors, and stairways are unmarred by time.

When I last resided here I was attending a wonderful wisdom school—a school where the mysteries of the Sacred Mother are taught. Barbara Hand Clow and many others studied there with me, but I do not remember what our names were then. After we completed our initiation, we chose to leave our home here and enter into form on the beautiful but troubled planet, third from the great sun known as Helios.*

Transitioning into materiality caused me to become forgetful of many of the ways we moved and thought here, but we had known that would happen and many arrangements had been made to assist us before we left. I will explain those as we move through these ancient halls. We understood, in that momentous decision we made after our initiation, that despite the limitations we would experience in human bodies, despite the unknown perils we could face, we would be creating a new and incredibly precious habitation where the Holy One would truly walk in the garden of delight intended from all eternity. And so we joyfully leapt into flesh. But now I have returned to the Pleiades, and my life on the turquoise planet we call Earth is something I will speak of in a moment.

And so we begin the tour of this marvelous house. There are presences inside, even though they are not apparent at first. To understand the peaceful, gentle nature of the Pleiadian homeland, it is necessary to realize that it is a climate generated of unity. Once we have passed through many initiations

---

*Helios is the personification of the sun in Greek mythology.

and have arrived at the state of awareness that destroys all veils between realities, it is clear that there is only the One.

Then manifestation of plurality becomes a playful way of life and there is no end of possibility. Just a twinkle of a perceived need or desire creates the "other" or "others" to fulfill it. This is not a trick or a summoning of zombie-like creatures to serve us. It is simply a mutual spark of recognition that it is "time"—but not time as we understand it in form. We know the others and they know us. There is simply a flow of the One and the All in the experience here, once we have transcended earthen consciousness.

Respect and privacy is a natural rhythm here. We would not consider disturbing the rest or the work of another until a certain spark leaps among us. Of course, this is simply inadequate language to speak of things very difficult to describe.

As we approach the entrance, there is a gradual shift from the expansive outer surroundings to the inner. A lush borderland of open green with lovely paths for meandering, wonderful old trees, flowers, and pebbles lead us to the interior without any pronounced divisions of space. Nothing about this house is excessive, although it is huge. Each room is fully functional for its purpose, and all of the space is delightful in design.

As we enter from a smallish sort of foyer, we find to our left a large glass atrium. In the center is the eternal Fountain of Living Water. Surrounding it, with backs to the fountain and hands outstretched, are thirteen goddesses, present in holographic form. They are not physically present here, yet they may touch and be touched. These are beings who are currently embodied elsewhere but keep a constant and conscious presence here, encircling the fountain. They are dispensers of grace and mercy, lending their essence to the Earth Mother Planet and her creatures. On Earth they are sometimes known as *boddhisatvas*—enlightened (*bodhi*) beings (*sattva*) motivated by great compassion.

Their names cannot be told, for they step in and out of this place as they perceive the need and their own desire. There is always one to take the place of another. I myself had a turn here and perhaps may choose to serve again. We always greet these presences upon entering the house, knowing that we are entering into their essence of rest and revitalization, kept alive by their warm heart energy.

To the right of the foyer is a structure of hand-cut stone shaped much like the atrium. It feels ancient and infinite, and in its center is a forge with an eternal flame. Large windows hewn in the stone are open to air and light, so there is no sooty damage to the old stone walls. All around these walls are hung imposing hand-forged swords, twelve in all. Their weight and the splendor of their craftsmanship make it clear that no human hand could support them. They, too, shift and change place as their owners, presently in form on Earth, leave them here while on their missions. How they came to be placed here is a mystery that will be explained as we continue.

The might and power of each sword is held here as a talisman of strength and a receptacle of honor for the god who used the sacred forge and anvil to personally shape it before placing it here. Now he is using his physical form as a smaller version of this instrument, this plan, this word he will speak, the muscle and intention that keeps him related to the larger weapon that is still his, still available to his hand. We always bow to these presences upon leaving the house, knowing that their fiery inspiration accompanies all of us and activates our brain energy.

The foyer itself is small, dark, and intriguing. It is initially difficult to grasp its shape and purpose, but it is the portal into all of the rooms in the house on every level.

Straight back is the Gathering Room—not huge, but important. In the very center of this chamber is a live vortex, the Blue Spiral. Its source from above cannot be traced, as it is lost in the suffusion of light flowing in from the transparent ceiling. It needs no opening, for it pierces the ceiling as a laser might. This is pure energy—the energy of the future as it connects and blends with the past.

The past is not past history, as it is usually understood, but rather it is our roots. From here in the Pleiades the Spiral burrows deep into the foundations of Earth and finds its connection only with what has passed through the alchemical fires of the Great Becoming to become eternal. The eternal is one—past, present, and future—and is drawing to itself all that *is* and all that *lives*. It is sourced in unknowable fields of light, and it reaches to the most hidden depths of reality.

The detritus that we have known as "past" is not a reality; it is swept away like dead grass of the fields, never to be remembered. All possible futures are distilled from the material forms set free by this passing on and letting go. As the Spiral turns, pure essence is released into the expanding cosmos. Our own transformation is central to this process.

The Gathering Room is not named for groups of beings

that meet here; rather it is the place where we gather the fruit of our human experience and bring it forth to the Spiral. We do not experience direction in the Pleiades, but this room honors the six directions of Earth—north, south, east, west, above, and below—and embraces them in the larger experience of the All.*

The gathering process that takes place deserves special explanation, as it is the key to all your earthen labors and every kind of experience. The Spiral is a vortex that reveals the fifth dimension and others beyond. It holds all of the four-dimensional experience of Earth, and only in that encapsulated experience that is the present moment is it possible to commune with beings and places beyond. Initiates come here after passing through the foyer and after greeting the immortal presences of the goddesses. They are prepared, then, through song and story to enter the energy of the Blue Spiral. This energy may be peculiar to the Pleiades. This scribe does not have knowledge of the wider universe, but she does know (for she has been prepared and instructed by wisdom teachers from many galaxies) that the energy of the Blue Spiral is part of a much larger energy system that flows through the undivided membrane of the entire universe. This scribe experiences the totality as the Living Body of the Cosmic Christ—that aspect of God that is present in all of creation. Other beings may choose to name it differently, but it is an eternal gestating, pulsing, conscious

---

*For more on the cardinal directions visit https://sites.google.com/site/colorsofthefourdirections/lakota. Most traditional people add two other directions: the blue of the Great Spirit, Grandfather Sky, and the green of the Divine Woman, Grandmother Earth. There is a seventh direction as well, the inner, most sacred of all.

expression of love/wisdom that animates all of life everywhere.

In the Gathering Room, initiates honor the six directions they have known on Earth by momentarily gathering all expressions of each one into awareness and renewing their bonds with them. Then, having absorbed and accepted all experience into themselves, they place themselves, one at a time, into the center of the Spiral, surrendering themselves and all that has touched them on Earth to the larger life of the Eternal. This is a form of communion, a sacred participation in the great metabolism of life.

Once a soul has consciously participated in this ceremony, it is connected forever to the Christ and receives its "diamond body." The denser body has been shed; that heavier dross that we cannot help but collect while in those first bodies has been released to be transformed into light. The precious gold of earthen experience is forever received into divinity. This has been the Great Plan all along. All material form is being transformed in and through our lives. Each of us can then embody a subtler form that is able to live on with less limitation and greater awareness. The one who is now able to show you these rooms, this mansion, is able to do so because she has taken part in the ceremony and has given over the older, denser body to live in the slightly more subtle new one. This is your heritage, as well.

We shall leave the house for now, pausing to honor the presences of the gods in the stone hall, as we go forward to continue building the Earth. We shall return here to the Pleiades very soon, for there are many other rooms yet to behold and lessons to learn in each.

TWO

Earthen Child

Long, long ago I was a child in a very earthen reality. I enjoyed the love and hospitality that all young beings should know from a caring set of grandparents. My consciousness was localized, as is the way in material form, in a place called West Philadelphia. It was a very ordinary part of a very big city during the Great Depression, and the adults of that place were suffering deeply.

But in a tiny spot within that larger milieu, we children found the portal that kept us connected to our Pleiadian homeland. It appeared to be what was called a "vestibule," an archaic name for a tiny enclosed foyer at the entrance to the house. That was where I underwent my first level of initiation while embodied. It was the entry level to the world of make-believe. We children dreamed up endless scenarios there. Sometimes it was a grocery store where we could come and exchange our homemade paper money for pictures of food and other products cut from magazines. We could afford anything we wanted there.

Sometimes it was a rocket ship preparing for takeoff and we shivered with anticipation. And at times, yes, we discovered some of the secrets of gender differences when we played doctor there. In darkness when we closed the door, or in daylight when left open, our imaginations were set free to soar. Many children, no doubt, achieve the same results when they drape blankets over dining room chairs to create a fort. Short periods of voluntary enclosure, when balanced with other sorts of play and activity, seem to generate creativity.

Little did we suspect then that we had stumbled into the foyer of the house in the Pleiades! But our creative imagination was being honed for our work of building the Earth, work for which we had been sent. We were learning to use imagination to form mental images or concepts beyond the senses, which would be useful in resolving difficulties. This is the most precious treasure we can attain—the ability to co-create with the power of God.

At the adult level, the need for enclosure in order to shape and mature our creative imagination translates to the need for reflection, meditation, and contemplation at varying times and according to the needs of the embodied soul. As we practice the discipline of silence and solitude, always in balance with other activities of work, study, and play, we finely hone the engine of the most powerful force earthlings can know—the creative imagination. That place we go is the portal to the beyond. When we have honored the space long enough, it will begin to give up its secrets and usher us into ways of knowing and being that have the capacity to build a newer, greener Earth, the one we have been sent to tend.

The enclosed space is not only the vessel of the sacred, it is also the cauldron in which the essence of material life simmers and stews until it reaches its fullest capacity for joy. Inside it, appearances often seem turned inside out, so that we begin to see the Creator's plan shining through the molecules of biology and geology that dance with the Divine. This type of adult play, first introduced in childhood and known in Jungian psychology as "deep play," refers to the inner work done through imagination and amplification of mythological and archetypal material. When we have been blessed to see the truth, we begin to use the imagination to craft that which we know to be possible. We return to our roots in eternity.

THREE

The Pleiadian Experience

Knowing that all images are parts of the divine holism that is life, it will not surprise you now to see that the foyer in the house in the Pleiades is not made of brick or stone or glass, but of organic material, grown from its roots in the Source. It is the stem of a glorious and living white rose. This is why the house cannot be approached from "outside" the organic oneness. It simply *is,* and all who come to know it, know it from inside, through that "foyer" or portal they find within themselves.

As we continue now to explore the first floor, we begin to notice a very slight slant in the floor. As we climb to higher levels, the leaning toward the center will become more evident. This is clearly a multidimensional house.

There is a library here that holds a lush secret. It contains comparatively few volumes when one considers all the literature of all the ages. Just the known writings are beyond comprehension! Nonetheless, the wisdom of all the ages is here, if one knows how to unearth it. I will speak more about that as we look around the house.

This small archive has more than books lining its inviting

shelves and nooks. There are images covering its walls, all relating one to the next in a pleasing display. Some are placid, calm images, others are puzzling and/or disturbing images, but none of the images depict the Holy One. No snapshots or great works of art pretend to be the final capture of the holy reality. Most of the art simply displays life in its flow, as it is in its every expression.

These many expressions of the face of reality, fashioned by brush or pen, have been donated to this room by initiates passing through the Blue Spiral who were willing to lend their talent and consciousness to the all. By using their gifts for the good of all, they allowed these precious extensions of their humanity to be brought to this place outside of time. Here they are glorious in their transformed and eternal form. Here they are maintained as in a gallery that will forever record the passage of Earth through its epic voyage in materiality. The ones who will come here and study the great works, the great patterns that the artists of Earth have worked out, will be enriched beyond measure. It will help future explorers to tease out the threads and patterns of all cosmic life.

Soft, comfortable chairs are available in every small nook for those who would like to sit and gaze, read, or just contemplate. Square wooden tables with hard-backed chairs are placed for those who wish to write, study, or just doodle.

There is one among all these chairs that has amazing powers. I won't describe it to you because if you visit there, you must be led to that chair by inner guide or intuition. It can be found only by one who is ready, in which case the chair is also looking for that person. Yet it will seem just an insignificant

THE PLEIADIAN EXPERIENCE   13

piece of furniture if you accidentally happen to sit in it.

This chair is known mystically to all cultures, but in kabbalistic lore, it is called the *merkavah*.* This is the main reason why this library needs no great horde of books; it holds all the truths given to all the worlds through its connection with the merkavah. This is the famed Flying Chariot that can transport a passenger through time and space. This seat can take you to the great library of ancient Alexandria, to the halls of the Akashic Records,† as well as to sources of wisdom, past and future.

This is the one and only secret that I will not pass on to you in this account. It is a secret that can be discovered only along one's own unique pathway, or not at all. No one can teach it to another, because it is the search itself that does the teaching. It is in our very uniqueness that we find the entrance to our oneness. Anything less than full embrace of our own purpose and power fails the quest. Let that be the only clue given, for if you can read these words and follow, you can find the way to the time machine on your own.

The kitchen beckons us with aromas both familiar and strange. This is the hardest room to reconcile with the rest of the elegant, serene surroundings. But it should be remembered that we are no longer in Kansas (or Katmandu). This

---

*Also known as *merkabah*. Some early Jewish mysticism, c. 100 BCE–1000 CE, featured stories of ascents to heavenly palaces and the throne of God. The *Maaseh Merkabah* (Works of the Chariot) was a significant text in this tradition.

†The Akashic Records (from *akasha,* the Sanskrit word for "sky," "space," or "ether") are a compendium of mystical knowledge believed to be encoded in a nonphysical plane of existence known as the "astral plane."

amazing room is really a laboratory in which experiments are always "cooking."

Here Cinderella stands beside the fireplace sweeping cold ashes, participating in a drama that may lead to her future happiness. She is gambling that by following her unique pathway she will discover a partner for her heart. She has left another place in the starry heavens to come here following her dream.

Brother Lawrence* quietly stirs his soup and spends his generous spirit feeding his fellows while practicing the presence of God. He is concentrating on the secret he has learned so as to teach it to others who do not yet understand their own divinity. He understands that only the present moment is real.

Jesus and a few of his friends are seated at a rough-hewn table, eating heartily with unwashed hands and chuckling over some private amusement. They enjoy this place in which there is always a warm welcome and a place to rest for a bit.

Suspended above an immense stone hearth in the center of the room is a great black cauldron. The fire is tended by a young boy who is supervised by a hag. One look at her and you realize you are in a serious laboratory that helps to move the heavenly bodies. You know for certain that if she pleases, she can pop you into her cauldron and dissolve you in its bubbling broth. Or she can just as easily bless you with three drops of her potion upon your tongue and make you immortal in a

---

*Brother Lawrence of the Resurrection (c. 1614–1691), a lay brother who worked in the kitchen of a French Carmelite monastery, was believed to have an intimate relationship with God. It is described in a text compiled after his death, *The Practice of the Presence of God* (Merchant Books).

wink. Few people return there once they have met Ceridwen,* but for those brave enough, the real quest can begin in this place.

Perhaps you will risk entering that kitchen with me later; it took many years of my life on Earth before I was able to and permitted to enter Ceridwen's rich kitchen, and you will find your way there when it is best. For now it may seem safer and easier to begin, as I myself did in my novice years, by going up the stairs to the second level of the mansion.

The lovely winding staircase is quite wide and wrought of polished ebony. I was intrigued by its air of mystery and went directly to the rooms above, before returning to explore the lower level. Each of us does it the way that is best for us. However, there are places, such as the merkavah in the library below, that will not be discovered for all our touring until we have awakened to the timeless truth of this house: it is our own.

And so I began as most do, examining what seemed to be a quaint and gracious mansion. On the second level the incline of the floor in each room is slightly more pronounced, and although noticeable, it is easy to ignore, because it is disconcerting to the balance we have known on Earth. We neglect, at first, to ask the questions that would reveal more than we are ready to know.

Along the less-than-straight hallway are many, many rooms, each unique in palette and style but all comfortably furnished

---

*The Celtic goddess Ceridwen was alleged in Welsh medieval legend to have swallowed her servant, Gwion Bach, who was then reborn through her as the poet Taliesin. In the Wiccan tradition she is known as the goddess of rebirth, transformation, and inspiration.

for guests, who stay as long as they desire. These rooms have a special enchantment about them that the uninitiated seeker finds compelling. The pull of the charm becomes more pronounced with each room.

Some seekers have no conscious idea of why they have come. Others, such as I, have a deep and burning hunger and feel more at home with each step. But each of us finds, as we make the rounds and gaze at every room, the one that draws us most strongly. Like Goldilocks, I found the one that was "just right" for me and instantly fell upon the inviting bed and into a deep sleep.

The house knows how to welcome each seeker and lead us to the place we need to be. I needed rest and enclosure in order for my true essence to begin to gather and grow strong. Later I understood what happens on this level, and I will explain it now, in case you find yourself there.

This is the Hall of the Initiates, and here all beginners on the quest begin their "becoming." The white rose that is the house has captured them, as a lover captures the beloved in a net of delight. The irresistible fragrance we instinctively follow is the first memory of the homeland, and it is right to follow its scent and be lured into the great dreaming.

These dreamers, while just novices at first, are the future of the entire universe. Only in their dreaming, having put aside for the moment all hectic agendas and striving, do they become citizens of the new Earth, as she takes her rightful place in the all. She will no longer be a silent, isolated planet in the lonely void, but a vital part of the exchange that takes place among the worlds.

Only in this place of dreaming do we learn that connection and begin to learn our role as co-creators of the web of life and love. We come here to our initiation through the stem of the rose that is planted on Earth and reaches up to our mansion in the Pleiades and beyond. It is part of the natural evolution of earthlings into divine beings, manifestations of the One being.

Outside of time I slept on, while on Earth I followed the busy routine of a military wife and mother of six. Each of my experiences of womanhood was a chapter in the dream happening elsewhere. I cooked, cleaned house, shopped, laundered, kept appointments, studied, read, primped and groomed, loved and learned, nurtured my little ones, prayed and worshipped, led scripture studies, and wrote my emerging theories in countless journals and letters to friends, all of this activity unfolding in its own way in the Hall of the Initiates.

I had entered not only the vibrant stem and petals of new life but also of real and eternal life that would make my earthen experience something that the entire web of life could know through me. Was I aware of all that as I busied myself with countless tasks and responsibilities on Earth and slept my charmed and blessed sleep in the Pleiades? Of course not; like everyone else, I learned only through the journey itself. Eventually I had to go back and visit all the levels of the mansion, including those I had skipped as well as those I had not begun to imagine existed.

Since my story cannot be told in a linear fashion, I will tell you about my visit to the third level next, although we will have to revisit it in its turn. This is what happened to me as I awoke from my rest on the second tier and began to move higher.

From the second level the staircase grows ever narrower and there is no railing, only walls to hold onto for support. It is not frightening in the usual sense, but there is a sense of isolation. It is evident that these stairs are not often used, and it engenders a sense of entering into alien territory. Only the fool or the child keeps on, feeling the draw of something or someone that must be known. It feels more important than anything ever has.

It's not entirely obvious that this liminal space is "between the worlds." It is not entirely unknown territory, nor is it hostile, but it is no longer familiar. I began to lose a defined sense of identity; new thoughts began to invade, thoughts that entered unbidden, yet had a ring of eternity about them that made them feel more solid than my former ways of thinking.

Some of these thoughts began to feel like memory, and I knew I had been in this place before. *Am I right now one of the people on the second level dreaming that I am awake and climbing these stairs? Am I actually dreaming myself to a higher level? Which am I—the dreamer or the climber? Who is drawing me to this higher place?*

As I approached the third level it became more and more difficult to think these questions or even to think in the same concepts as before. I seemed to be losing the thread of what had appeared to be so sure a reality on Earth. The perfumed essence became stronger and began to be the only reality. The walls no longer guided my hands, for they had vanished and were unnecessary. Questions seemed to dissolve before they were fully framed, and the atmosphere was saturated with peace.

The Grand Hallway now appeared at the top and the stairs ended there. It seemed to be the final level in this old house. In the Grand Hallway stillness prevails, yet there is a vibrant sense of active participation in something very alive. It is as if unseen presences are keeping some sort of machinery humming, some sort of garden flourishing, some sort of celebration alive with dancing and color. In my still earthen body, changed though it had been already, I could perceive worlds being born; minds crackling with creativity; hearts bursting with redemptive love; lovers exploding in the fulfillment of union; children leaping; women soaring; men laughing with joy; insects buzzing and building; birds flying, swimming, and nesting; animals large and small sunning themselves, romping, and stretching their muscles; crocuses reaching for the light; lilies trumpeting their delight; and the very dead leaves of earth plunging downward, settling deep into her embrace, offering themselves to transformation as they become coal and then diamond, resplendent forever.

All of this I knew and felt, yet all was still and without strain or doing of any kind. How could this be? What is the secret of this place upon which I had stumbled? This house I thought was mine had become ours. Of course it always was, but I had come back to my home in the Pleiades now and was able to remember that. All of the cosmos lives in this home in the Pleiades with me and with you. I/we do not need to move any of its parts; we only need to be one and many as we are moved by the Great All.

I strolled along the Grand Hallway past many doors, all ajar. On the outside of each door is a full-length mirror, and I gazed into one after another of the mirrors, without entering any of the doors. In each mirror I saw another facet of myself. One-by-one I passed each door, moving toward the far end of the corridor and seeing in turn a juggling clown, a crawling toddler, a pony-tailed cowgirl, an executioner in a black mask, a butcher separating a joint of meat, a cab driver bent over the wheel, a willow tree bending as if to salute me, a mother in a desert country reaching out a bony hand for bread for her emaciated child, a comet rocketing through space, a near-frantic emergency room doctor, a teenage boy in Middle Eastern garb lovingly cradling a violin, and a large salmon breaking the surface of the water to stare blankly at me.

I scanned both sides of the hallway as I walked, seeing and wondering. Then I returned to my position at the top of the stairs, passing each doorway again. All of the faces had now changed! A white buffalo calf morphed, as I watched, into a beautiful Native American woman.* A shy young boy transformed into a Tibetan lama before my eyes, and an ancient tree became in a twinkling the central axis of a great world. There were ancient runes inscribed on one mirror—an alphabet that seized my heart and almost took my breath away. I knew that in that room lay the bard Taliesin, and if I so much as peeked inside I would go to him and lie down in his arms forever. The pull was so sweet and the longing so overwhelming that I had to force myself to move on, sending my love to sweeten his dream. For his sake as well as my own I needed to keep moving for now.

---

*The legendary White Buffalo Calf Woman is the primary sacred prophet of the Lakota religion.

Each door, each mirror, revealed a memorable, living presence that needed to be acknowledged and thanked. I realized that sleeping behind these doors were all the masters, whether garbed poorly and simply as the poet Jalaluddin Rumi, Mahatma Ghandi, and Mother Teresa, minister to the poor; clothed in sandals and tunics as Joan of Arc, the Sufi mystic Rābi'ah al-Baṣrī of Iran, and Brother Francis of Assisi, patron saint of animals; or robed in fine garments and jewelry as the Shulamite woman from the *Song of Songs* and King David. Out of love or from curiosity I could easily have stepped in to be with any of them. But not one of them is the Great All, and I resisted the urge to rest there.

All are dreaming the universe into being, maintaining its rhythms. That is the deep flow of activity I sense, one that pulses through the entire house. Their dreams are filtering down to the sleeping initiates below, finding niches in each one where they can grow like seedlings finding fertile soil. The initiates actually identify their correct rooms by aligning with the room above to best catch the seedling, along with its inspiration for growth. Each finds correspondence in kindred souls, and the entire Earth and all the worlds are fertilized through that process.

I had two reasons not to enter these rooms, so much more pointedly curling their petals toward the center: First, I had not the right to interrupt any one of these interactions, which are so profound and essential. Second, I had not yet ascended to my God and your God, so as to be given my own role and my own place in this great alchemy. I dared not stop at any door until the one that was mine would be opened to me. As

I reached the stairway again, finding no place else to go, I was startled to find an enclosed alcove I had not noticed right at the head of the landing. It slowly opened to reveal an elderly couple. He wore a long white robe embroidered with pomegranates and edged at the hem with tiny tinkling bells. She, too, wore a long white robe, but open in front over a garment the rosy color of dawn. On her left hand was a wedding ring, unassuming but stunning. It was of the lightest spun silver filigree and bore a simple inscription: "God alone." I read it in English, knowing it was the seal of her marriage covenant with the Holy One. I wondered if all seekers could read it in their own language.

That caused me to look at *his* left hand, where I saw a beautifully crafted ring that featured a tiny, living white rosebud at its center. On his right hand was a signet ring, whose seal I could not make out for the dazzling light it emanated. These two are the guardians of, and the presence in, the Ark, which I had mistaken for a simple alcove in the wall. In a sudden flash of brilliance, laced with the most tender love, they spread immense wings I had not seen until then. They took me into their embrace, and I disappeared with them into the Ark to become something new. I cannot tell now how long I slept in their embrace. The brilliance of the light within the Ark of the Covenant* has both consumed and enhanced my

---

*The Ark of the Covenant is a chest described in the book of Exodus that was built at God's command in accordance with instructions given to Moses on Mount Sinai. Hebrew nomads built a tent to house the Ark and carried it with them everywhere they traveled, understanding that God dwelt in their midst. This is an earlier intimation of incarnation—God's presence in a material container.

individual consciousness. There is no way to speak of sequence in the usual sense, for there is neither time here nor space. Yet I know that, in the turning of the great wheel, there has been movement.

I have never left the light, this home, or their embrace. But I have awakened within it, lived and served, fallen asleep again, dreamed, and waked again. And I have remembered the dreams!

FOUR

Memories of Earth

Sometimes I remember the lovely and gracious turquoise planet where we create the drama of the One and the many. That world is such joy, despite the tendency we often have to create negativity and darkness. We have not yet learned to remain in form and remember our oneness. The natural beauty of Earth surpasses even the dream that created it. I bow my head in reverence and awe that she has permitted the full breadth and depth of that terrible and tender drama to be enacted upon her.

She is a rich garden of possibilities in which living beings can experience all the crises and sensations that material form imposes on reality. The many facets of the One are sensing and tasting every extreme of her depths and heights, her deep ocean trenches, her desert wastes, her frigid mountaintops, and her fertile valleys. They experience the molecular structure of the soil in which they crawl, labor, and reproduce; enjoy the fruits of that labor in bounty; and suffer its droughts. They know the satisfaction of a full belly, the agony of starving progeny, the raw terror of being the creature that must undergo digestion by another.

She has agreed to be the bringer and nurturer of life, even as the very life she bears scars, gouges, and disfigures her in its immature blindness. Like greedy young animals, we sometimes look only to what we feel we need and do not notice the mother we are using as an object. She knows this is the way of new life. The mother tree in the forest lives only for the nursling, as the human mother spends herself for her child. She hopes to bring the little ones into the respectful, contributing, generous community of the larger life as they begin to understand the true symbiosis of planetary existence.

Earth must feel and witness the unmitigated tragedies, as well as the ongoing thrill of ever-new celebrations of love and remembrance. Nothing, not the smallest movement of the great life she holds, escapes her awareness. She continues to say: "Let it be done in me according to your word," for it is the One that she is birthing into ever-greater fullness. It is she—Earth—that holds the title, with great honor, of Theotokos—the God-bearer.*

With one heart and one mind we have understood the brutal and ecstatically beautiful task that is asked of her in bringing forth what has been called "the human condition." It would better be called "the material condition," for all of life-in-form shares the burden and the potential.

One man who was sent to her understood well the

---

*Theotokos is the Greek word for "God-bearer," a title that was granted to Mary, mother of Jesus, by the Catholic Church as acknowledgment that she bore God into flesh when she birthed Jesus.

dilemma presented to her and to all matter. He even realized his own culpability in the stark and devastating result of this experiment in physical form. Trembling at that moment, with blood flowing like sweat from his very pores at the presentation of this cup for his acceptance in time, as it had been accepted in eternity, he asked that the cup, the earthen experience, this agonizing participation in materiality, be taken back. Realizing the totality of the cost to each of us, he asked for the plan to be abandoned if at all possible. Brought to his knees in the experience of our vulnerability to physical and emotional pain, he wished to give back the cup of our becoming—the vessel of our mingling with divinity, the Holy Grail of our wholeness in God.

But this place, this round bowl of the cup of earth, is the cauldron in which life is subsumed into greater life. And he bowed his head to that greater knowledge, despite the moment of hesitation. And we, too, knowing the cost, bow to Earth and to all her children, both the courageous and the greedy of all forms.

During my time on that mysterious orb circling Helios, I often forgot the rhythms, the embrace, the breath of the All. But I was never alone there; we are never alone, there or anywhere. The many were and are breathing our every breath, feeling our every heartbeat and footstep.

We sift the sand on the beaches of Earth through our mortal fingers and the immortal All knows for itself the feeling of silkiness, damp grit, and sea air mixing with the molecules. The heady smells and evocative sounds of crashing surf or gently lapping waves become reality to the Creator of these worlds.

We who take on form immerse the very spirit of life, the One, the Source, in the experience of matter.

Even as we voluntarily provide this knowing to the All, we ourselves are most often unable to experience the original oneness, for to take on form is too often to feel exiled in separation. We yearn and grieve over the loss we have not truly suffered.

But the beings of light attend those of us in mortal form, and the sensitive among us can detect their very subtle movements. We can choose to become more and more aware of these stirrings from within and without. Thus we begin to awaken, despite the dense nature of physicality. As we awaken by degrees, their light penetrates deeper into our form-bound biology and teaches it a new way of existing. Until we become aware of this gentle blending, we remain clay that is still inert, still resistant to rooting new life.

God did not breathe life into clay in a garden of long-ago eons; at some point we realize that this breath of life is ongoing. It is a relationship between God and the creation, so intimate that the holy breath sustains it in every moment. The beautiful images in scriptures of every religion are meant to help us realize our profound intimacy with the Holy One. It is an ongoing tending of the life planted in the earthly garden.

The divinity is right now breathing life and spirit into dense physical matter, loosening the density of the structure that would keep it lifeless. While you and I are in form, the creation of the cosmos is continuing. We ourselves are co-creating, with the Holy One, a new creature we have not yet imagined. As holy breath penetrates the matter we now are, it becomes lighter, richer, and deeply fecund. It is another way of imagining a pregnancy in which Earth herself is gestating the child of spirit. It is the marriage of spirit with matter that takes place through the intercourse of receptive matter with Holy Spirit. The promised child to come, the Emmanuel of prophecy, is this child gestating in us as we awaken and take on light.* The image of Mary's pregnancy with Jesus is meant to teach us how God is conceived in human flesh. Extending this to all of creation, we can see that the prophecy of Emmanuel is meant to lead us to the evolutionary meaning of what it is to bear God in flesh as a planet.

Evolution on Earth is a process of breathing the God-life into an ever-new manifestation, more subtle and less dense. Outside of time, in what has been called the "pleroma"—the fullness or totality of divine being—God holds that wonderful image of the perfected creation within the inner chamber of divine love and knowledge. In that place that is not a place, but an ecstasy of being, the experiment/relationship is complete and perfect. It—we—lives within the bridal chamber of that perfect love and ecstasy with the godhead.

This is a loveliness, a majesty, that the All can gaze upon and that has been called "heaven," for inside the awareness of that blessed state of Beatific Vision† there is nothing to be added or desired. Because we are one, perfect totality with the

---

*Emmanuel (Hebrew for "God is with us") is both a symbolic name and biblical prophecy in Isaiah 7:14 and Matthew 1:22–23.
†In Christian theology, the Beatific Vision is the ultimate direct communication of God to an individual.

All, we participate more and more, even in form, in the bliss and ecstasy of that vision as we awaken to our true "I-dentity."

We have been given an image of this state of perfection, this object of God's complete and continuous love that over-shadows our humanity and its material form. The image given is of the young Jewess from Nazareth who was chosen by God to bear the "first of many sisters and brothers" of the new consciousness. That is what was truly being announced by Gabriel, the angel of incarnation and a frequent direct messenger from God in both the Bible and the Qu'ran. In the Gospel of Luke, Gabriel appears to the virgin Mary foretelling the birth of Jesus.

Mary of Nazareth, a human woman, is recognized by the Catholic Church and most Christian churches as the "Mother of God." In the Catholic Church she is called "The Immaculate Conception."* What does this actually mean for the future of the human race? It means that we have been given an image—a picture—to study until we have become mature and awake enough to see that immaculate conception means an eternal conception, the perfected outcome of all the Earth. There is no other name that suits this pattern of God's love for creation so well. It expresses, in both the microcosm that is Mary and Jesus and the macrocosm that is the entire cosmos, an eternal gestation held in the heart of Love itself. The story of Mary reveals to us that all human flesh is sacred and in a mysterious

---

*The Immaculate Conception dogma of the Catholic Church holds that from the moment she was conceived in the womb of her own mother, Mary, was free of original sin. It refers to the conception of Mary by her mother, Saint Anne.

manner is even now being assumed* into union with divinity.

The more we allow spirit to moisten, fertilize, penetrate, and loosen the rigid feeling, thinking, and acting functions of the entity we believe ourselves to be, the more this truth rises on the horizon of our awareness. We are truly fashioned from very dense clay of earth, and anyone who tries to plant in clay knows that it is difficult to penetrate. It is hard to dig in and to find space for a young seedling, and tender young shoots have a difficult time reaching and spreading in order to grow. The clay needs to be aerated, moistened, and mixed with more porous materials. Then we have the "good soil" that Jesus spoke of in his famous parable of the seeds. It is quite amazing that spiritual seeds are able to grow at all in the cement-like clay of the earthen mind/body.

We begin to see, little by little, if we are gently nurtured and fertilized, that this plan of immaculate conception—a plan held in God's mind for all of us—is what all ages have looked forward to as heaven. It is not necessary to depart planet Earth in order to live in the bliss and unity of this blessed vision. Many of us travelers have entered into the sacred bridal chamber and seen for ourselves, although there may be far more to enjoy when we have completely left our dense bodies behind and become bodies of light. Physical death does not guarantee this blissful outcome, nor does physical life make it impossible to experience.

---

*The Assumption dogma of the Catholic Church holds that the Blessed Mother did not die but was received body and soul into heaven, to reign there as queen of heaven and earth. It reinforces the ancient belief that the body is sacred and is intended for immortality.

I will have more to say about the necessary purging each soul endures in order to come into that beatific state, but it can be completed on Earth or after the soul has departed the body. For now I must return to the tour of my current residence in the blue islands of the Pleiades.

FIVE

First Awakening

I was gradually awakening to find myself truly inside the Ark of the Covenant, within the holy container where God has chosen to pitch a tent and dwell among us, inside the embrace of the sacred marriage that crosses our DNA with divinity.

I suppose I had better pause and elaborate on my choice of words here. How does one (God or creature) "dwell" within a sacred, or any other type of, marriage? And how is the Ark of the Covenant, sacred to so many peoples of the world, a marriage?

Long ago, our fellow humans living a desert life knew that their God accompanied them wherever they moved, dwelling in a special, elaborate tent they had constructed for him. According to the stories, at times the "glory of the Lord" could be seen hovering over the tent, a temporary dwelling that was suitable for their nomadic existence. When the cloud of glory lifted, the people knew it was time to move on. God was thereby leading them to the promised land, where they would build a permanent dwelling for the Lord.

The temple at Jerusalem was an elaborate affair, but served the same purpose the tent had served. Deep inside, in the "holiest of holies," a place where no one but the high priest could set foot under special ritual circumstances, God still dwelt with his people. It was known that inside the Ark, the Shekinah—the feminine counterpart of Yahweh—dwelt with him in eternal embrace.* This is where and how the "holy presence" lived among the people. Two golden cherubim—outer symbols of the inner mystery—hovered there with wings touching.

Is that *just* an ancient story? Or is it a projection of a place in our consciousness where the holy mystery still resides? Is the most inner mystery of our humanity, the secret that is so closely guarded and protected, the everlasting marriage of divinity with matter that is constantly being celebrated within us? Do we just imagine such things? Or does the intuition of millions of souls who have walked this Earth tell us of a truth that we have not yet grown into knowing? Are we really the offspring of God's love affair with matter? And do we live and move within that embrace at every moment, aware or not? Are what appear as separate earthen, clay bodies really seamless tents of flesh that move with us wherever we go, containing, revealing, and also concealing the mystery of the sacred marriage at all times?

I will relate, as best I can in the difficult language of Earth (in every tongue), my own unique remembrance of those moments. In time and space our attempts at communication are clumsy. When the heart is finally freed from all its

---

*Shekinah, in Hebrew, is the feminine ancient blessing of God. The original word means "dwelling" and refers to the dwelling of the divine presence of God, especially in the temple in Jerusalem.

impediments, it speaks a truer and richer language that leaps between souls, but I will do my best to translate the things that happened.

I use the phrase "my own unique remembrance" because we of the One are not a collective with a hive mind, even though we have an unbreakable connection in the All. We are as diverse and unique as your lungs are from the hair growing on your head. We are highly differentiated beings with unique gifts and abilities. But we are One. Diversity and freshness are, in fact, hallmarks of the Holy One. Eternity is, in my personal and unique understanding, a bliss of discovery among us. Because of our total uniqueness within a perfect unity, each of us may find heaven, or eternal life, to be quite different, yet always harmonious and fulfilling throughout the All. Just as we co-create our experience in form, bringing forth that which we are capable of creatively imagining, so the life we experience as eternal is co-created from our highest level of creative imagining.

When I first entered the house I have described as a novice, the house I later realized I had never left, I went directly up the stairs without pausing to examine the first-floor rooms. I couldn't see why anyone would do it any other way! I was swept directly into the intrigue of the lovely old staircase and had a deep need to climb and explore. I even marveled at how easy the climb seemed to be and how quickly I discovered the wonders inside. I was truly lost in the drama and glamour of having been permitted into this hallowed place. Having at last found myself welcomed into the circle of love that was the old people's embrace, I actually believed that I had entered into the final state of conscious union with God. I could not yet understand, in my naïve desire to know God, that my own love was still pre-love, or in other words, love that served itself more than it served the beloved. I had a very long way to go yet, and many lessons to learn.

What happened to me at that time was like a near-death experience, although it was strictly a psychic happening. From within the warm, loving cocoon of the sacred couple's love, I was shown that I had to go back out into the world to learn what the other levels had to teach me and, eventually, to share my discoveries with others. I was reluctant to return to the unknown, but there was no thought of refusing; it would have been a betrayal of my own immaculate heart. I went forth with my pockets filled with treasures for the rest of the journey.

SIX

Descent

I descended the stairs again, with each step feeling heavier and more aware of my own being, a weight that did not exist in the higher realms. Remembering intellectually, but without being able to feel the connection any longer, I tried to shape my thoughts, feelings, and prayer into the ways I felt I "should" be behaving. The more I tried to regain the experience or control my feelings, the more entangled I became in the heavy, meshy "me."

Forgetting that I had agreed to come back for a purpose, and that unseen multitudes were supporting me, I fell into the illusion that I could judge my worth by the performance of my work and/or prayer, things that did not seem to amount to much in my eyes. I began to believe the lie that I was separate from God and from all the possibilities I had dreamed of becoming. Even more painful, I fell into the belief-stupor that I myself was somehow responsible for the terrible breach. I had fallen into the error of thinking that a separated self could even breathe or pray without the grace of the divine connection.

I remember that the One called Jesus had told us we were like branches connected to the vine and that all life comes to us through the vine. Cut off from it, we would have no life. For my own good, my soul was allowing me to make the attempt to "do it myself" so that I would learn the humility and delight of being part of the divine flow of sap that keeps us all alive and fruitful, even when we cannot feel any of the sap moving. It is one of the most difficult lessons to learn in our mortal form.

In this way of confusion and doubt, I descended the narrow, dark stairway past the sleeping initiates in their snug chambers, wondering why anyone would climb that far just to dream. Dreaming itself began to seem like a dangerous occupation, something that led only to this dark illusion I was in. *How long,* I thought, *must I wander in this cloud of ignorance before I break free from this fantasy and into the bright sunlight of the "real" world?*

It seemed many long ages before I came to understand that there is no real world other than the one that grows organically from the mother soil, whose garden of life encompasses the entire cosmos and was not primarily designed for the comfort of the seedling. Our beautiful, turquoise gem of a planet is a root-bed for the glorious rose in its fullness. Each seed must grow through hot sun, refreshing rain, winds, storms, and infestation by insects. Each must die in time, so as to return its elements to the spiral. All of those elements go on to live and die again and again as the great alchemy simmers on in the vast cauldron. The process is so immense and beyond our mortal perception that we can only learn to trust the Mother Planet herself to know what is best in each season.

But all of that was yet to be understood as I churned in my worry and doubt, in fear that I had somehow, without

knowing how, missed the boat. This makes me recall a wonderful observation of the late mythologist and teacher Joseph
Campbell, who reminded us that there is no boat. "We are," he
said, repeating a Polynesian expression, "standing on a whale,
fishing for minnows."

More out of real ignorance than any ill intention, I wanted
to hurry up the process of achieving sainthood, because I
thought God would be able to use me better if I were better.
All of these goals are so misguided, since it is always the process of living that is itself the goal. The true "I" is not an isolated self that can achieve anything or do anything of itself.
But I had not yet learned that simplest truth. I wanted, at the
time, to skip the steps in between and bring myself to perfection, so as to please the Great Gardener *more than any other
seedling!* How selfish was my love for God, stemming from my
own human wounds and needs.

All I could find in the "me" was sadness for my lacks and
yearning for what I perceived to be missing. The greatest and
kindest lesson that ever came to me was to learn to die well and
completely, a skill I learned from a talented and very spiritual
therapist, Dr. Bonnie Damron. Lovingly, she taught me the lesson of the chrysalis. Perceiving that I was stuck between worlds,
as truly I was, she accompanied me on the journey and reassured
me of the need to allow the death process to complete itself.

Up until then I had "died" many deaths, but like trick
birthday candles that can't be extinguished, I popped right
back up each time, still "me" and ready to continue the fight.
Of course I speak here of the death that must come to the
smaller self in order for a larger life, a fuller participation in

eternal life, to begin. I could never get the hang of letting go.

This wise woman encouraged me, once "dead," to moulder in the grave, to decompose, to allow myself the rotting and stinking process, the annihilation of true death. It was not quick or easy. But like the caterpillar, the person I was had to dissolve in the chrysalis. This is the only true alchemy, and the Master Alchemist alone can supervise the work. It is not a do-it-yourself project and can't be learned by reading or hearing about it. Even the caterpillar cannot learn it that way. True decomposition is a process that, on Earth, usually takes years. And since we humans are not caterpillars, we have other work to do even while cocooned.

So this process must go on like a soundtrack in a movie that others barely perceive as the movie unfolds. It runs in the background of life and only the person in the chrysalis can perceive it. It is an attitude of yielding the "me" to be "ground like wheat," as earlier spiritual writers have told us. We allow ourselves to be "crushed like grapes" into a wine that can flow through our connected larger self and can perceive the connection.

Opening ourselves to that connection is opening ourselves to the awareness and fuller life of the vine. That is the secret to eternal life, because, once aware of the connection as an organic, constant flow, we are in our home. It does not matter whether in form or not; we are in our blissful home in the universe and in whatever worlds that may include forever.

There is an important distinction to add here. Allowing the ego to be transformed is neither a matter of getting rid of the ego, nor is it an excuse for any self-inflicted suffering.

A healthy ego is our way of doing the work and making the relationships that are so necessary to building the Earth. It is our best friend, but it is not our essence. We work, pray, and cooperate with grace to teach our individual egos to be strong and serve the greater self. The small ego is not the king, queen, or center; it is the champion of the One. As it becomes transformed, it embraces this task with joy, seeing, as the young Mary did in Nazareth, that it is a most blessed choice.

And so I have digressed, but life itself digresses constantly to visit the necessary nooks and crannies of its own experience. It is a journey of surprises, some necessarily painful, some joyous, and some glorious beyond words! But this detour in words was not a detour at all, for here we are about to tour the house again, with eyes that can see more clearly.

SEVEN

A Second Look

We enter the lovely glass atrium of the fountain and know now that these goddesses whose earthen bodies are serving elsewhere are often unaware, as you and I are, of the incredible presence they are holding here in the wonderful house. As they labor, discover, suffer, and triumph on Earth, they knowingly or unknowingly firmly hold their center here at the eternal fountain. As crystal cups poured from the great fountain of divine love, they hold the essence for all who would sip of it.

I was amazed and humbled at this mystery, this majesty, this secret of our humanity hidden in the ordinary moments of time/space. And I was renewed. Lifted above my selfish desire to be perfect, I began to embrace my human frailties as part of the story of earthly existence. I gave gratitude for my own femininity that I share with these sister beings.

Having knelt before them and given true reverence, I left the chamber to enter, again, the Hall of the Swords. Still the ancient forge dominated the center of the old stone room, and I marveled once more at the strength and handicraft of the enormous weapons lining its walls. Each one unique, each one mighty, they were reminiscent of an unseen presence of true valor and honor.

Suddenly a young man entered the chamber and without seeming to detect my presence, went straight to his work. What took him years of his life played out before my eyes like time-sequence photography. I watched him heat the raw steel and begin to yield it to the fire. The work was exhausting as he heated the huge blade and withdrew it again and again, testing and retesting it. The youth became a mature man as he worked and as the weapon became stronger and more massive. I watched his stature grow to match the mighty heft of the sword as it grew into a spectacular finished product.

After many, many seasons of his life that flew by as a flash in my vision, the sword was complete, unique, and totally his. He had become a master and a giant. Easily he lifted the beautiful instrument to its place on the hallowed wall, reserved only for him. Then, humbly, he withdrew.

As he saluted the others and then left the hall, I saw him as the man he had now become—mature and steady, but otherwise like all other men in appearance. I knew that when he parted from the sight of that sword, he would have moments when he doubted his achievement and other moments when he felt himself to be too small to wield its great power. Yet I also knew that from its place in that holy house, the sword would continue to radiate its power through him in all his endeavors.

Once again I felt a surge of joy at being part of this amazing fellowship of humanity. I understood that through him and with him I had a share in the connected energy of every sword hanging there. Giving thanks and reverence for the dedication of so many, I saluted the others and left the hall knowing that my life, too, was extremely valuable. I was energized and challenged to take on the work of building Earth, without needing to see the "me" or knowing the fruit of my work.

Back in the darkened foyer I felt the cocoon-like comfort but was also more aware of the fiery charge of the Earth's core pulling me with magnetism, pushing me onward with electric intensity. I sensed a depth under my feet that I had not yet explored and I looked upward, past the lovely stairs and the shadows of the narrower passage above it. I wondered how tall and deep this house could possibly be. I had not yet become acquainted with the underground chambers, nor with the top level of the house, which I later came to know quite well.

Seeking to counter the dizzying sense of up/down and push/pull, I moved toward the kitchen. I saw that Jesus still lingered with his friends around the huge, rustic, welcoming table. Timidly I moved to join them and was welcomed as an old and dear companion. Surreptitiously (I thought), from the corner of my eye, I checked his hands and those of the others. They were all fresh and clean as newborn babies, except that on his there lingered a bit of caked blood from a tiny, still-raw wound in each.

"We cleaned up in your honor," he smiled, and several of his male friends winked at me, while the ladies present just rolled their eyes. I was abashed, but could feel so much warmth and kindness present that I sat down immediately to the feast.

Once again, there is no way to calculate how long I lingered with them while devout prayers were offered, food was brought forth, songs were sung, jokes were enjoyed, and bread, wine, tears, and laughter were shared among the whole company. Finally he got up and told us he had an important task to do and would not see us for a while. But before he hurried out, he whispered into my ear, "I will see you again, for I am going to prepare a place for you."

I wondered at his words and a pang of loss clutched at my heart, but he was gone.

With the group breaking up, I looked around to find Brother Lawrence, who went straight to work preparing a wonderful, delicious-looking pudding. Instinctively I knew he could tell me how to comfort my grieving heart.

"I have heard of your reputation for mending hearts and souls," I began. But he already knew what was ailing me. "You *will* see him again, as he said," he smiled.

"But how will I know where to find him?"

"Stop looking back to where he was and do not look ahead to where you think he will be. He is with you in the moment, if only you don't miss it. If you fail to find him in the *now,* you will never do so."

"But I am here now and I don't see him," I protested; "he has gone!"

"Only because you are looking at me, child! Stop looking outward and look for him within."

I thanked him, not really sure what he meant, but from the corner of my eye I caught a flash of fire. I turned quickly to see Cinderella kindling a new fire in the huge old fireplace. Expertly she fanned the small flame into a roaring, leaping blaze to warm the whole room. I had many questions to ask her, but she was already hurrying to other tasks. Catching up with her, I asked if I could talk to her and she just said, "Come along!"

I began to pitch in, helping her carry soiled laundry to be washed and ironed, cleaning up spills, mending and polishing, all at a feverish pace. We scarcely had time to breathe, much less carry on a conversation. Finally she paused briefly to show me something. She took from a secret closet a lovely dress that shone like the sun and seemed made of moonbeams held together by stars. She held it close for a moment, caressing the gossamer material, and then replaced it, locking the cabinet. In that small pause I asked her, "Is that the dress your stepmother will wear to the ball?"

"Oh, no," she smiled sweetly. "It is my own dear mother's dress. I am keeping it for my marriage one day."

"Ohhhh . . ." I was very impressed. "But if you possess such a gown, why are you working as a servant?"

Again she smiled sweetly, "This gown is of another world and cannot be worn in this one. But it makes all my work lighter to remember that dress. As you help me with my work here, you and I are bringing that other world into reality in this one, so that one day we can both dress like queens."

I was flabbergasted. "We? Do you mean to tell me that I will have a dress like that, too?"

"You already do," she assured me. "You must go on now and leave me to my work while you do your own. Each of us will dream and work until our dreams become a part of a larger world. But they already exist in the Pleiades. Have you forgotten?"

My head was spinning by now. I had thought I was in the

Pleiades, inside the wonderful house. But Cinderella had said
. . . what? She had spoken of her love for her beautiful mother
who was never far from her thoughts. She had dazzled my eyes
with a dress I couldn't believe was possible, yet it was not hers
to wear in *this* world. What world were we in, then? Her words
intrigued me and I began to wonder where my home was. I
envied her such a mother who would leave her the legacy of
that dress, and I longed deeply for my own mother. Perhaps if
I could find her, she would have beautiful objects to share with
me.

Deep in this quiet longing, I moved on.

From somewhere near the pantry I heard sobbing and
moved toward the sound to find a young boy who seemed
inconsolable. "Can I help?" I asked the lad.

"No one can help me now, for I have lost my father and
will never see him again," he said miserably. "It was my fault
because I was foolish and ran away from him—the only person
who loved me and cared for me." His sobbing broke my heart
and I found myself weeping with him.

"I don't mean to make things sadder for you, but I have lost
my mother, too, so I really feel your distress," I managed to say
through my sniffles. "Maybe we can look for them together?"

"That would be easy for you," he said, "because you are a
real woman with a body, and arms and legs that move. I am
only a puppet who cannot move by myself."

"Sometimes I feel like a puppet," I offered. "And I think
you look a lot like a real boy. I think maybe we could manage the quest if we decided to be very strong and help one
another."

At that he stopped crying and cocked his dear little wooden head at me, as if he'd just remembered a wonderful thing. "There *is* a fairy," he started, "but she is probably very angry at me because I did not listen to her. She probably would not like to help us now."

"Have you asked her?" I said hopefully.

"Well, no, because I am so ashamed of the very, very bad thing that I did."

"What have you done that is so bad?" I asked.

Timidly he hung his head and replied, in a tiny voice: "My father wanted me to go to school and learn to become a real boy. But instead I went away with some people who only wanted to use me for their own good. They promised to take me to Pleasure Island and I believed them, because I thought it would be more fun than going to school . . ." His voice trailed off as his little painted eyes began again to brim with tears.

I felt so terrible for this child who had been tricked and could not have fully understood the temptation that came to him. He really believed it was his own fault and that he had betrayed his father. His grief was so pitiful to watch that I soon forgot my own.

"Tell me your name, please," I asked. "My name is Mary."

"My father named me Benjamin," he almost whispered.

"We will go on an adventure, Benjamin," I promised him. "We will find your father *and* my mother. When your father sees how brave you are, he will know how much you love him and he will forgive you. You'll see! Now let's go find your fairy and ask her to help us."

Neither of us had any idea where we would begin our search, but we began to march out of the kitchen, spirits and heads held high.

Suddenly, just as we were nearly out of that place, two strong hands, like claws, picked us both up and plopped us unceremoniously, like live lobsters, into her huge, steaming cauldron. Just before I disappeared in the foaming, scalding broth I saw Ceridwen's eye, without a shred of pity in it. She cackled at me, "Looking for a fairy, are we, pet?" and watched me sink below.

Good fairies come in all shapes and sizes. Whoops! The words "nice" and "good" have really nothing to do with each other. Those were my last thoughts as my companion and I dissolved painfully, another lesson to learn as the unforgiving broth became richer for the addition of its new ingredients.

With the flesh melted off my bones and unsure of how or what I was, I became part of the soup and our adventure had begun. Only one who has been cooked alive in the soup will understand what I am about to say. On the other hand, if you find yourself understanding what I am about to say, it is assured that you have been cooked alive in the soup. Perhaps you just did not recognize that at the time.

My little friend and I existed in a time out of time for as long as it took until we lost the illusion that we were two. Inside the great cauldron, with my life dissolving around me and his separate life dissolving as well, we honored his father's wishes and took ourselves to school. We sat at a desk in a college classroom in the time/space continuum of Earth. "We" went on to graduate school and earned a master's degree in psychology.

During all this time of cooking, brewing, and transforming, the two of us became one. We became stronger and wiser and he became a real boy and then a strong man inside the container of our adventure. No longer were either of us puppets, but one more complete being within the All.

EIGHT

Inside the Cauldron

Now I must tell you where the little boy's father had been during all this time. Perhaps, if you heard the story of Pinocchio as you were growing up, you may have guessed that the young puppet's father was a cobbler named Gepetto. But the "puppet master" is a far greater image than that of the man in this one story.

By now you must suspect that the cauldron into which Ceridwen had so unceremoniously dropped me could also be perceived, in other meaning systems, as "the belly of the whale." The biblical Jonah was neither the first nor the last to be torn from his moorings and tossed to the mercy of the elements.* The Master Alchemist is a genius at the great work of blending and transforming our raw essences. It is an opus that separates us from the material-form illusion of having distinct ownership of personal privilege, status, and drama.

Jonah's mistake was to believe he had a choice about

---

*Jonah is an Old Testament prophet famous for being swallowed by a fish or a whale. The biblical story of Jonah is repeated, with a few notable differences, in the Qur'an.

accepting the purpose for which he had come into form. He was called by God for the sake of All. He was to warn the people of Nineveh* and give them an informed choice about whether or not to cooperate with the help God was sending to them. Jonah had to learn that to save them was to save himself. To ignore his special calling was also to destroy himself. It is all a lesson in perception. We truly are One. We accept the "callings" we receive so as to be in our place in the All—a place that no one else can fill. The things that seem to be taken away from us are only being given to us in new ways, as we are blended into something/someone far, far greater than we had understood ourselves to be.

At times these lessons come to us in a gentle touch, and other times they come like a cuff from a mother bear. Love is stronger than death, and as strong as it needs to be to bring the beloved to consciousness. It brings the beloved out of the clutches of death and into greater and more abundant life in whatever way is necessary. For, at the core, it is our own love that loves us more deeply and more steadfastly than any other love could. The great love abides in us and among us and is Emmanuel. This is the Promise of Ages—a promise that we will all come home to the love that *we are*.

So my friend, the little puppet, and I had been searching, questing, learning, and becoming integrated into one. Ceridwen stirred us and sang over us, dissolving and re-forming us until, eventually, we came to find the place inside that cauldron where our father was trapped. Our larger story began when we

---

*Nineveh, capital of the ancient Neo-Assyrian Empire, was the largest city in the world for about fifty years.

realized that we had been brought into that stew pot to find other missing pieces of ourselves.

Sometimes it takes quite a bit of tossing about in a place where we can find no footing, where the waves of circumstance threaten to drown us, before we can let go of the smaller vision we hold of ourselves and our heritage in the wider universe.

We found our father, as I will shortly explain, in a ship that had foundered in that deep, watery place. Many are the travelers who lose their way in such a mysterious ocean. Some count too heavily on a ship that gives them false confidence, and others try to make the journey without help and fall short of the strength they need. A very wise poet, Leonard Cohen, wrote: "And when he knew for certain only drowning men could see him, he said all men will be sailors then, until the sea shall free them."

The waters were becoming more peaceful and the sun began to be visible through the murky depths; the youngster with me had become a strong and human part of myself. Together we had performed the task that was necessary for our intellectual and societal development. We had escaped Pleasure Island, which for me had been a place of denying my own scholarly abilities and needs in order to please others in my life. I was finally able to see how this attitude of needing to please had crippled and stunted the young, masculine side of myself. And as I was about to find out, we were products of a puppet master who surely meant well, but only knew how to raise puppets.

It was just at that point when we came upon the ship. It had become a prison, now, for those trapped inside. As we felt its cold, rusty deadness, we understood that our father was one of those unfortunate prisoners. How in the world had this happened? There was no time to consider that question; we searched with our hands for a door, a gate, or a lock. We found the lock, and inside it we found an ancient key, all but crusted over and unrecognizable from centuries of neglect. We worked it slowly free and swam upward, following a weak beam of light.

Standing on top of the sunken wreck, we broke free of the watery grip for a moment. There was no land in sight, and the sky still roiled with the last of the gray clouds breaking apart. In that moment I felt a nudge—a surge—of raw power I had never known before. With faith and trust in the One, and in a burst of pure exhilaration, I lifted the decrepit key high over my head. A piercing ray of bright sunlight answered my gesture and shattered the remaining cloud cover. It was more electric than a lightning bolt, but harmless, as the intense energy flooded through me from head to toe, and with a convulsion of sheer joy I heard these words spoken to me: "This is my beloved son, in whom I am well pleased."

The force of energy coursing through my body transformed me, and the ancient key had become new and golden again. I knew that the first part of our search was over and a new one was about to begin. We had the precious key!

The freeing of our father from the prison ship would take many more years to complete, as it turned out, but at least we had found him. Once inside the vessel we swam joyously to his side to tell him the good news. We had to navigate our way through dead bones, slime, and poisonous waste material, but finally we found his cell, deep in the lowest holds of the ship. At last we burst upon him, ready for a joyful reunion.

The years of living without light and air had taken a great toll on him, and he shied away from our approach. Uselessly we related to him our adventure and the things we had learned. In a voice cracked and dying, he told us that we were wrong and upbraided us for our foolishness.

"This is the way we are meant to live, he insisted. It is the Creator's will, and we have no right to look for another way. We will be rewarded for our suffering and patience someday."

"But this is that day," we proclaimed. "The One has sent us to free you!"

It seemed to us that the miraculous journey we had just survived was proof enough that we had been sent. How could he doubt it? It seemed that despite our good intentions, we were only causing him more pain. He growled and turned away from us saying, "I will remain here in the ship."

It was no use trying to change his mind, and it seemed to us that any attempt to remove him by force risked breaking an already frail bone. So in great sadness, we left him.

This was the final lesson that Ceridwen wished for us to learn at that time: despite the truth we now held that had set us free, we had no right to impose it on another who wished to cling to his own truth.

With a quick swipe of her slotted spoon she removed us from the kettle. We were seasoned and toughened now, no longer easy fish bait.

It was time for us to serve our first turn as initiates. We had nearly forgotten our lovely home, yet here we were again in the marvelous kitchen.

NINE

The Initiation

Quickly we were brought to the Gathering Room, where bards and storytellers from many worlds awaited us. We sat captivated as, one after another, they sang their songs and epics and wove the enchanted fabric of story. We felt as if under a spell as we became woven into the story itself—that great song of becoming.

Tales we had never heard began to sound familiar as the characters and places, the challenges and tasks, the sad or happy endings rang familiar chords in our memory. We began to understand that the patterns are all a part of the great pattern by which life knows itself.

When the enchanted song and speech subsided at last, we knew clearly what was expected of us for now. Thrilled beyond measure, we rose and entered into the Blue Spiral so splendidly alive in the room. We circled into the great cyclical pattern itself and gave up all of our adventures, trials, sadness, and even our inflated delight in our achievements into its wise turning. In love and surrender we were brushed clean of any clinging desires and glamour about the outcome of the stories. They

55

belonged now to the eternal experience of the All. Something of us—of me—had become eternal in the All, and the One was beginning to take flesh in this mortal frame.

As we stepped forth from the Spiral, we were led to our differentiated tasks, which did not separate the new awareness of our unity. I was led to the Atrium of the Living Waters while my counterpart was led to the Hall of the Swords. No longer would we stay physically in touch at all times, as we had been, but each of us would be completing the work of the other in the All. We were, in fact, no longer male or female, nor young or old, but we lived now in the Christ, the Anointed One who had been sent.

Benjamin moved directly to the sacred forge. He looked in awe, for just a moment, at the fire, while he picked up the raw steel.

I moved toward the atrium where one of the goddesses greeted me, invited me into the circle, and handed me the cup that would now be mine to hold as I dispensed the water.

The "time" I spent at the glorious fountain is a fond memory that I sometimes wish I could recapture. It was a very necessary step in my preparation and development, so I will explain how it felt to be in that privileged position.

To stand at the inexhaustible fountain and receive its waters into your own hands is an intoxicating delight. It means that while you are still in your mortal body, living an ordinary or extraordinary life on Earth, you become aware from time to time of the presence you hold in that other dimension that seems to be outside time and space. The promise that Jesus gave to the woman at the well—that a fountain could well up from within and keep you from ever thirsting again—has taken root in you and you drink from it constantly, with enough to overflow into the lives of others.

Whether the world around you sees it or not, you are aware that the living water is flowing through you and deeply touching other lives. It heals, and refreshes, and renews. People receive gifts of strength and understanding, faith and mercy. One knows that the spirit of *all life* has become available and abundant in the world. One also feels sure that this is a new experience overtaking the whole world and that soon all people will be able to share in this bubbling flow. Soon enough, however, we start making plans for God in the way *we* think it should happen. That always means another learning time is near.

After months or eons of what would be Earth time, a smiling young woman approached me and held out her hands to receive the cup. I let her drink of the water, expecting her to then move on, but she remained in a gracious, receptive posture until I realized she was ready to receive the cup itself. She reminded me so much of the younger, purer self I'd been on the day I stood in her position. So I stepped away, relinquishing the vessel and allowing her to take the spot.

The song of another earthling poet comes to mind as I write these remembrances:

> *There's a time for everyone, if they'd only learn that*
> *the twisting kaleidoscope moves us all in turn.*
>
> ELTON JOHN

Stepping into the small foyer, I was overjoyed to see my

young lad, who had finished his work, too, and become a mature, middle-aged man, sturdy and graying. I knew that if I looked, I would see a handsome new sword shining in its place on the Wall of Champions. Benjamin and I embraced warmly and went to find our next adventure.

Two things took place that are worth reporting back to you: The first is about the disorientation we felt at being taken from the work we had begun to understand as our role. Perhaps we had not yet fully integrated the idea that we are not a "role," but a spiritual reality that *is*. To step away from that task when it is time is frightening and sometimes painful, because it asks one to believe by sheer faith alone that one has a task at all, anywhere.

The second thing is the continuation of the Pleiadian experience and the deeper exploration of that on which we then embarked. These two things took place in a rhythm of sunshine, rainbows, storms, and hurricanes—in other words, during everyday life on Earth.

Removal from my place at the fountain meant that "charity" toward others could no longer be my everyday experience. The charity I felt before was not yet the true virtue that proceeds directly from the heart of the Divine. This is a most difficult feeling to lose when we have been following the will, mind, and heart of the spirit as well as we humanly can for a long time. We have been trained in compassion, and it is difficult to understand why we are either unable to feel it or are mysteriously restricted in some way from our former habits and reactions of giving and loving. This happens in myriad and very personal ways to each of us, as we can manage it. It seems as if we have lost our compassion, but only the feeling of it has been taken away temporarily, so that we learn to care without the good feelings it brings. Then eventually, if we yield to the stirrings from within in the new ways we are learning, we can gradually see that "we" have no power to love or serve "them."

This should not be misunderstood or used as an excuse for callousness. It is a right, proper, and holy thing and a necessary step in our spiritual growth to use our best human gifts, values, and resources, along with our highest attributes, in the name of justice; and to love and protect our fellow creatures. The urge to sacrifice self for the good of others bears and has borne great fruit for our small planet. Those who have given in small or large ways, even to the extent of giving up their lives, are inspired and supported by that fountain of love from within, even when it is not recognized. But gradually we learn that the others are not "other" and there is no longer any need to think in the old ways.

Therefore, when that urge to pity or affection is withdrawn from our feeling level, especially after we have known and responded to it frequently, we may be taken aback and terrified that somehow we have "lost" the way. But there is a time for most of us in approaching union with the Divine when, for a brief or an agonizingly long period, we are mysteriously incapable of feeling human compassion. This does not mean we offer no compassion, but the offering is now coming from a very different place that does not concern the ego, and it is often given without the person's understanding that it is happening. It is a very painful time, whether long or short, but a necessary one in order to learn that it is not "I" who loves, gives, and nurtures, but rather the "I" that is eternal and is, simply stated, the All loving the All—not "others."

So what is the difference? How does the difference matter or make any impact on the people, flowers, and fauna—the many expressions of the Source abounding on the planet and in the cosmos? How can one small person, one small cell of life make any difference at all?

As the veils are permitted and encouraged to drop, the illusion of separation falls away and the fountain is found within; it is no longer something to be approached. Once it is experienced from within, there can be a turbulent tossing about due to the lack of comprehension. You may feel loved or not at first, but yet feel as if the world you knew is upside-down or there is no firm ground underfoot.

This is the same imagery that Saint John of the Cross* spoke of when he attested that God's light is so bright as to be a darkness to our untrained eyes. As we first enter into that closeness and lack of separation, we enter into disorientation.

We may feel singed by the fire or totally immolated in the sacrificial burning away of the sense of self we knew previously. Giving up the familiar sense of separation can often feel more like dismemberment than union. But total union, total "real-I-zation," is the opus of a lifetime and can take ecstatic, glorious, terrible, and exhausting representations to the small being that is busy being inundated with reality.

We may feel flooded with devotion and great charity

---

*Saint John of the Cross was a sixteenth-century Spanish mystic, Roman Catholic saint, and Carmelite friar. His poetry and studies on the growth of the soul are renowned in spiritual literature.

toward others, but that is not yet the full (never final) state of union with the beloved. There comes a time or many times of overwhelm, of drowning, of true panic as reality surrounds and inundates the smaller being that does not yet understand its own smallness, its limitations, its captivity in the illusion of separateness. We may even feel, at times, more separated than ever. If there has been a sense of closeness to God (in whatever tradition that term is understood), that is often the most difficult thing of all to lose. We must lose it for the very reason that it, too, is an illusion, not yet the state that truly *is*—the union that really exists. As long as we feel close to the beloved, we have not yet experienced oneness. Therefore we may feel tossed about, rejected, at fault, burned, or drowned—all of these interspersed with moments of high inspiration and deep love. It is very difficult to hold onto equanimity or balance when the former norms of equanimity and balance are shifting through transformation. But we are being guided and gently moved into a new balance entirely. It is a balance of peace that finally prevails when we find our place within the All.

As we look back at our father's reluctance to leave his prison cell, we have great compassion, for what he was doing was choosing to remain in a role where he could "know" that he was serving God, rather than abandoning that place for the sea itself and the unknown of the greater depths. Why should he take my word for the wisdom of that decision? He made his decisions based on what he felt were tried and true (Piscean Age) principles. Yet there he was, deteriorating in ways he did not really see. We all do what we really believe to be best for ourselves, and who can challenge that position?

However, for those who have the insight and vision to move on, we will find that the individual is fashioned in union with the will and mind, the beating heart of the living, breathing All. The "how" of that happening will forever escape those who seek a point of beginning, because the Source is beyond any contemplation of separation. It knows itself only *now* and only as it is (or as *I AM*). It loves only what *is,* which exists only because of that ever-living love.

If God is not "born" in me, is not brought fully to realization, then how can God live and have agency on the planet, in the cosmos, in my neighborhood, school, home, or business? The difference between acts of charity toward others and acts done within the mind and will and heart of the All is that the latter have no human limitations or self-interest of any kind, and truly benefit *All that is* in both seen and unseen ways.

While these lessons are being assimilated, slowly and in the midst of distress, we feel ourselves to be in a limbo state. Eventually it passes.

TEN

Discovering the Fourth Level

Meanwhile, back at the wonderful house, Benjamin and I were still exploring. I had come to understand that there was a fourth level and that it could actually be detected from the outside if one looked at the house sideways. But the Grand Stairway ended on the third level, at the place where I'd discovered the alcove containing the Ark of the Covenant. Could it be that there was an entrance through some hidden room or corridor?

So up again we climbed, past the second floor and the dreamers, up into the narrow, darkening stair that still felt like forbidden territory. Again we slowly circled the corridor with all its rooms. This time I did not pause to examine all the doors. They were now closed, but I knew that many expressions of the All were taking part there in the Great Work. I wondered how that would feel and what would be the experience there someday.

We passed on, feeling along the old walls for a hint of something more. I remembered an image from a dream I'd had while still an initiate. In the dream I had found an opening in a wall high above my head. It had looked like an ordinary storage space, but had no obvious means of access. But I had been curious and had managed to jump up and grab hold of what seemed like molding. I had been able to push at the paneling till it opened a bit, and then pulled myself up and through the opening, tumbling to the floor on a whole new level.

It occurred to me that the dream might have been a memory, as so many things are. So I moved along the walls, jumping here and there, until I felt the edge of the barely visible molding graze my hand. Benjamin lifted me as I seized it, kicking and scrabbling to get a better hold so I could pull myself up to where I could push on the panel. Sure enough, it gave way to my touch and I found myself reliving the dream. I pulled him up behind me.

All around us were treasures—old and valuable bits I had brought with me here from the turquoise planet. I was truly amazed, both that I had forgotten the magnificent collection and at the strange variety of things that I had felt to be valuable and brought with me. Some seemed strangely mundane, such as the wooden baby highchair with built-in potty. It was both nostalgic and humorous that I should have treasured a thing like that, a thing I had no doubt used in the long ago. It flashed me back to a memory of West Philadelphia, planet Earth, circa 1938. Now those things were in a room that was not a room, but another world altogether.

We could not remain there for long—just long enough to realize that there was a wealth of material to explore. One of the first surprises of the fourth level was that I had brought many remnants of childhood joys, including at least three amusement park rides. One of my earliest memories of West Philadelphia is Woodside Park, where fortunate children went for picnics, outings, and rides on the attractions. How I longed to be able to go there!

So perhaps it is not surprising at all that in this place that is the "first of many, many mansions"—the "first heaven"—there is childlike delight.* I rediscovered a ride for toddlers that consists of a circle of small flying elephants (based on Dumbo). Only a child could fit in the tiny seats and go around and around, high up in the air (about four feet off the ground), mesmerized by a miniature version of the same movement as the solar system.

Another ride, designed for older children and adults, was a very tame roller coaster. The thrill in this experience was the illusion of danger in cresting the gentle hills and curves. It was quite safe but deliciously scary at times.

The third ride there was actually safer yet, but seemed to be the most frightening, because passengers rode in individual cars that disappeared into dark underground tunnels. Although every car was occupied, being out of sight created a feeling of being separate and alone in the passage forward into darkness and the unknown. As in other aspects of life, it takes courage to climb aboard, but one is able to see things in the dark that cannot be seen in the light. And after the ride, we know things about other types of sight that we did not know before.

---

*"First heaven" is a term adapted from scripture in the spirit of what St. Paul tells us of his experiences. It is meant to convey a state above the ordinary vision of earthly life, where we find the *beginning* stages of perfect peace and bliss—the fifth dimension.

In a lonely corner of the fourth level, a mannequin of an old gypsy woman will tell your fortune for fun. But it is a very impersonal "fortune," pre-written on a card, and it says nothing illuminating. It's easy to see it is just a lifeless machine. We have literally put her in a box and she can only dispense canned, premeditated advice. We long for the mysterious woman, gypsy or not, who can live and breathe, bleed and love, and give us warm, intelligent counsel based on her life's wisdom. In that sudden longing we remember our search for mother—the tender touch of her hands, and the scent of her skin and hair.

We explored that level lovingly and often, finding that its boundaries lay somewhere in infinity. There are parts of it I have not yet entered. I hope to be able to explore these still unknown dimensions with you as we go along.

Benjamin and I went back into the world of form after that sojourn in the house and we made a separation of sorts. He felt that he was called to do wonderful heroic things, picturing himself metaphorically riding a strong horse and making great changes in cultural patterns. I felt that I was called to quietly learn and teach about the ways of spirituality, so I studied some of the religions and great mythologies of the world to better understand what connected and what divided us. My children were growing up and passing into their own adulthood and new lives; everything was shifting in my life. Some of these young adults to whom I had given birth had major battles to overcome, and I was always caught up in the tragedies and the victories. There seemed no rest or comfort, except in the inner peace that came when I most needed it. I still meditated and prayed to the inner guide I now knew to be God. I had not yet really experienced the constant unity in which I now live.

I was, I suppose, in deep denial about the state of my marriage, which I'd always thought to be strong and unbreakable. Of all the things in the world that were most valuable to me, I felt my marriage was at the top of the list and that God would help us to keep it strong. I loved my husband deeply as best friend, lover, companion, and strong support for my well-being. It always appeared to me that he felt the same. However, we both knew that he was not happy and was always searching for something to help him overcome his depressed state. I just never imagined it might be me that he had to leave behind; that was an unthinkable proposition.

For about five years we struggled on, as our closeness diminished in unseen ways yet seemed to flourish ever more in other ways. I see no good that can come of delving into a past that no longer exists, so I will say no more about that time.

Meanwhile, I felt ever more clearly a need to teach the wonderful lessons I was learning. I used the occasions I could to create seminars and share the mix of spirituality and Jungian psychology that served me well and made so much sense in my life.

I felt ready to go to higher levels and further explore those realms I had begun to discover. Naturally I headed back to the wonderful house in the Pleiades to explore the fourth level. I felt sure I could, once again, find the hidden portal for entry from the third floor.

ELEVEN

Grandmother Spider

Lovely sconces were placed here and there along the corridor. I stopped to examine more closely the intricate design of one of these light-giving fixtures. A stray hair seemed caught between the edge of the round fitting and the wall. It seemed strange, since everything was so clean and tidy here. I pulled at it to remove it, and to my shock, it wriggled. Repulsed, I realized I had tugged on one leg of a huge black spider, which was now emerging into view. A great, horrible shadow had been hiding in the light, and I now had to face it head on. I was not prepared at all for this turn of events! I shuddered and fled as quickly as I could.

But everything in this house is mine and I belong to the house as much as it belongs to me. There is no way to escape what must be known and accepted. It was time to see what I would not see.

After a little time went by, I went back to face my fears. Summoning all the courage I could, I climbed the stairs and called out to Grandmother Spider* to come and tell me what

---

*Grandmother Spider is the creator of the world for the Native American Pueblo and Navajo peoples. In their mythology she spun a web, laced it with dew, and flung it into the sky, thus creating the stars.

she wanted me to know. Soon she came into view and mockingly invited me to come closer. "Won't you come into my parlor?" she asked, knowing I would recognize the childhood rhyme that foretells disaster for the fly.

I was somehow graced to see that this was the mother I had been searching for all my life. It is difficult to understand, but I can only relate my truth as I lived it. I saw through the disguise of her terrible, destroyer aspect and knew that she alone could give me my life. I accepted her invitation into the dreadful "parlor." Testing my resolve, she asked if I was sure I wanted what she had to give. With my knees quaking, I said yes—the most momentous and costly decision of my life.

"This time," she said, reminding me of my ordeal in Ceridwen's cauldron, "I will suck the very marrow from your bones!"

Probably very foolishly (for my journey is and has been that of the fool) I cried out: "I know who you are; you cannot trick me! Do you really love me that much that you would pursue me so?" For, in that moment I knew I was looking at the face of God and nothing else mattered except my love for her.

You must believe that this inspired moment was short-lived and that I later tried to plead that I had been tricked. But that would take a little time. The date on Earth was October of 2001. In New York City the previous month, the twin towers had just crashed to the ground, spinning our world into a maelstrom. And that month, in a country across the world, a new woman entered my husband's life and altered our family forever. I now know I had just given permission for this event to occur, an event as disastrous and final for my children and me as the end of the World Trade Center was for the United States. But I was not to learn the meaning of the invitation from Grandmother Spider until two years later.

Sadly, just before we would have celebrated our fiftieth wedding anniversary, my husband moved on to the new life he felt beckoning. We had come to the end of our road, something I had never dreamed could happen. We'd been closest of friends and dearly beloveds since I was age sixteen and he was eighteen. I could not imagine life without him.

This next revelation is the most difficult to admit and the most painful to reveal, but I share it as part of the necessary information of this transition through which we are all passing. That truth is that I had only one false idol in my life, a life that, in every other way, was dedicated to the Divine. That false idol was a deep and crippling fear of abandonment. Having been abandoned as a two-year-old child, it was a fear that inhabited every cell of my body. It was the last impediment to total union with the divinity that I know we all share, but seldom experience.

The way this played out was that I had come to cling to my spouse as if my life depended on him alone. It blocked the growth I still needed. Worse, I saw in the end that I had entrapped him in the spidery meshes of my needs and had begun to live my own life according to what I thought I needed to do to keep him with me. The marriage that had seemed so ideal was a hiding place for both of us. There truly was a dark shadow hiding in the light! The miracle of grace was to finally have it exposed.

Hindus understand the goddess Kali as the destroyer aspect

of God that devours whatever needs to be taken away so that life may go on and flourish.* Her appearance is dreadful, and Westerners would not ordinarily think of God with such a mien. But I have met her, have been devoured by her, and have lived to tell the tale of transformation that is her gift. Perhaps if you have suffered deeply, you may find resonance with what I have to say. I reveal such a very private and intimate experience only for the sake of others who may find some sense of purpose through hearing it.

At first I could not function at all; then I felt as if my legs had been amputated. I experienced a part of my body as missing altogether and a constant, unceasing loss of blood from the open wound where the appendage had been. It took many months before I even got to the point where I knew I had been metaphorically beheaded *and* dismembered. I would have to spend years collecting the parts and struggling to put some of it back together. Dream after dream showed me the wounds that were losing blood at an alarming rate. There were excruciating moments when I disappeared altogether from my own sense of existence, and it was only with the help of many dear friends and my loving children that I held onto the scraps of a life to try to rebuild.

In time—the infamous time that is said to heal all wounds, but does not—I came to learn that once I overcame my root of all fears, I would be truly free. As a two-year-old toddler I had lost my birth family; after my father abandoned us, my mother

---

*Kali, consort of Lord Shiva, is the fierce aspect of the goddess Durga (Parvati). She is the goddess of time and change, and although she sometimes appears dark and violent, she is an annihilator of evil.

mentally deteriorated. My two older siblings were removed to other homes, and so my loss was thorough and sudden. I was not aware for most of my young adult life of how this deep wound continued to vibrate in my being. I always felt I must overdo to be sure I was pleasing and "worth keeping." My constant fear, sometimes conscious and sometimes below the level of consciousness, was that the people I loved and friends I had would somehow discover that I am not good enough to keep.

This fear was totally irrational, for I was a good and popular friend and well accepted. However, I never trusted that I could maintain the seeming dichotomy between the person people thought I was and the person I feared I might really be. My life was one of outer tranquility and inner loneliness and depression. Never did I feel I could just relax anywhere. As I say this, I know I am speaking of a very common feeling shared by many people, but rarely voiced.

For me it is now very apparent that this deepest of all fears had to be shown for the lie it truly was. All fear is based on lies or misunderstandings of our own abilities and needs. We fall into beliefs that do not serve us, and then we are unable to serve the All in the powerful and ecstatic way we are meant to and to know that complete and undivided love.

Through all of this I prayed, begged, and pleaded to have our life back, but it was not to be. In every way that was possible without answering this prayer, God treated me as tenderly as a newborn child. I could not help but notice the many little reminders of love and presence all around me. However, this was not enough to help me to feel better yet.

In deep communion with God through contemplation, I

was learning the lessons of descent, so necessary for anyone who aspires to enlightenment. I had to be taken to the very depths of my humanity to experience the core that was Earth itself and also the center of the Godhead. The embrace—the deadly embrace of the Spider Woman—was the way down into the experience of total immersion. It removed all the obstacles that separated me from the oneness I had not yet experienced. I was one with the suffering of all people, as well as with the tiniest and most insignificant parts of creation. And in the end this became the root of my joy and the root of my new life.

Ten years passed between the day I met the spider in the hallway on the third floor of the mansion (just when I thought I was about to discover more of the marvelous fourth level, but instead was catapulted into the deepest dive of my life) and the time I began to recover and re-enter my life. At that point I felt as though I could go on and live a productive life again, but it seemed to me as if I had been permanently broken in some irrecoverable way. I felt my age more than ever before—I was seventy-five and did not believe there was much of life left to me. Still, I could smile again and enjoy family and friends. And then . . . I died.

In January of 2012 I contracted a sudden pernicious pneumonia in both lungs. I was hospitalized for seven full days in a state of weakness and illness that frightened my family and worried the doctors. I was not fully aware of the seriousness of my condition, although I was very sick. During the first hours after being placed into bed in the hospital room, I went through the death experience I will attempt to describe. I must truthfully say that none of the attending staff were aware I had actually passed over the line. It must have been very brief in linear time, but what I experienced was rather long and terrifying.

I did not see any lights, tunnels, or friendly beings, as is so often the report of those who have had near death experiences.* Instead I was taken to hell while still alive. This part of the journey was real beyond tolerance, and unendurable. Other than the illness, I felt no physical pain, but I was immersed in scenes of unbearable cruelty of one human being or more to other humans. I was unable to turn away or shut my eyes, even though I'm sure my physical eyes were closed in the hospital bed. No matter how I prayed and pleaded not to have to see, I was exposed to up-close scenes of the most bestial horrors. Over and over again I retched, as the brutality could not be endured. What made the events so terrible was that I knew beyond question that these were not imaginary scenes from a movie or from some distant memories, but were actually happening on Earth right then—happening in the moment right before my eyes. I cannot prove this statement, of course, but there was no doubt or thought of any kind except that I was witnessing a reality, not a dream.

After what seemed a full day and a half, this mercifully ended. I was then taken by what felt like two winged beings to a place that initially I did not recognize. Although I had never

---

*A near-death experience (NDE) is an event in which someone experiences the spirit leaving the physical body, and it is usually reported after an individual has been pronounced clinically dead or is very close to death. Sensations described include detachment from the body, floating, serenity, the presence of a light or lighted tunnel, and a bird's eye perspective of events taking place around the body.

read a real description of this place, I soon understood that it was the River Styx* and I was about to have my life entirely extinguished. The winged beings were holding me by my head and feet and were lowering me toward the repulsive swamp. I could see immediately that there was no coming back from this place of decay. Far from the fanciful river of mythology books, it was a sluggish, reeking, sulfurous yellow mud, just liquid enough to gurgle slightly as it barely moved. It looked like nothing so much as putrefied matter that would be toxic even to breathe. I was inches away and about to be dropped into it.

Some observing function in me was still operating, and this part was totally mystified by the situation and by my own behavior, for I was not struggling or fighting it in any way. The "observer" was thinking: *Surely this is not how God would have me die!* It made no sense that I would die and lose everything I had worked for in my whole life, since I could see that there was no resurrection of any kind possible after this. Yet the "other" part of me just yielded to the choice and said, *Oh well, if this is how it is . . .* right before I was totally immersed and blotted out.

Gradually I regained consciousness, too weak to even stay awake for long. I could only lie still in the bed and wonder what had happened. I was perplexed to find myself alive, but had no words to talk about the experience.

As I began to recover from the pneumonia and eventually left the hospital, I distinctly remembered this extremely real episode but did not understand what it was. It took weeks

---

*The River Styx in Greek mythology formed the boundary between earth and the underworld, or Hades.

and then more weeks as I began to understand the momentous thing that had happened. I did not tell the doctors about it because I was very puzzled myself about what had happened. Little by little, the facts sorted themselves out as I realized that it was another spiritual experience of transformation.

The waters of the Styx, it is said, cannot be collected in any vessel, for they dissolve anything that they touch. It is another way of saying that the impossible task can sometimes be accomplished. This task, for me, was to bring back from death the knowledge of the life beyond life, by allowing the vessel to be dissolved and resurrected. This seems to have been, for me, the definitive experience of leaving behind all brokenness, all past history, all sense of a former life and the beginning of life in the eternal now. I have, as I said in earlier pages, come back from death itself to bring my message of what one knows after passing over. And that leads us right back into the marvelous mansion.

Since my dip into the River Styx, a new life has taken over my entire being. Sixteen months later I was finally admitted further into the fourth level of the mansion in the Pleiades. That is where I discovered trunks overflowing with the fabric of creation. I have received almost constant guidance about the way we shall build the Earth together, using our own chaos to weave the future. It only needs sorting and dedicated weaving to create anew from what our planet has provided.

I have learned that fear is absolutely useless and that everything can be worked out from this higher level. I hope you will join me here soon and make the life-saving discoveries for yourself.

TWELVE

First of Many Mansions

In this world I now live in, this first of many mansions, it is possible to be in touch with the memories and sensations of the entire race of humanity. Just a tiny glimpse into the fourth level of this reality has reminded me of so many things that had seemed lost to our collective knowing. I will attempt to translate into human language the radiant and blissful secret behind our creation. It is time to reveal it to those who can receive it, for we are all on the verge of a great leap of ascension into our greater heritage and the knowledge of these momentous truths.

In the swirling mists and chaos of the unborn stars, in a world that was not yet a world, in a time before time, the One held an image that could, yet could not, be held. In the depths of the void that was not yet a void, in the bosom of a being that was not yet a being, there stirred order within the chaos. Beauty lifted its voice that was not yet a voice and cried out from within the nothingness to the heart that was not yet a heart until it heard the cry.

In that preverbal place that was not a place, word and

response found creation in one another. The image took on form, and the form was called the Immaculate Conception. Over the limitless abundance of the chaos, the image brooded until a something that could be known as a time and a place emerged, differentiated from the threads and scraps of the nothing. The being was now a being and the voice was a crystalline thing of beauty that brought forth the Word.*

> *In [what we call] the beginning was the Word;*
> *The Word was in God's presence, and the Word was God.*
> *[The Word] was present to God in the beginning.*
> *Through [the Word] all things came into being,*
> *and apart from [It] nothing came to be.*
> *Whatever came to be in [the Word], found life,*
> *life for the light of [created beings].*
> *The light shines on in darkness,*
> *a darkness that did not overcome it.*
>
> JOHN 1:1–5, NEW AMERICAN BIBLE

So far I have only begun to open and examine the contents of the wonderful trunks stored here in this house of the first mansion. Those I have opened cannot be closed again, for their contents are ready to come forth. They hold rich, sumptuous fabric. As if it is alive, it almost bubbles forth from the opened containers. In truth it *is* alive with the colors of saffron and roses, the cobalt of the deep seas, the tender green of new shoots, gray granites, sandstone reds and buffs, silvery whispers

---

*Since early Christian times, Christ has been referred to as the *logos,* which is Greek meaning "word."

of olive wood, black gleam of obsidian, and the almost-white of curling birch bark. As you can imagine, the colors are beyond counting or naming.

This is fabric left over, in the abundance of the chaos. The chaos continues to swirl until this very day. It has taken up residence here, within the field of creation, for it holds a treasure for us, still ready to be woven into more. Holy Love (for that is another name for the Self that found its being in the dance of partnership and ecstasy) used all the material needed to create the turquoise planet and its entire solar system, with Helios as its central star. The turquoise planet was surrounded with layers of protection so that life and love could emerge there.

What we must understand is that chaos is still a part of the earthen experience. But it is like the darkness overcome by the light. In each one of us is darkness and chaos in unbelievable proportion to our orderly, measured existence. In each of us is a darkness waiting to yield raw energy and material for ongoing creation. Each of us is invited now to open stored containers within ourselves containing enough material to continue to build the Earth and to go on to bless the silent regions of space. We will shine the light of our consciousness into this chaos, this darkness, and the darkness shall not overcome it!

For eons to come the children of Earth, daughters and sons of the sacred marriage of divinity and matter, will build and create the promised new heavens and earth and spread the message and joy of oneness throughout the galaxies, when we have learned to unlock the stored material, the marvelous love-fibers encoded in our DNA. All the answers, all the elusive little steps of new technologies and new sociologies, are already there. So how do we begin to find the treasure chests and the keys?

If you have read this far in my own adventure, you are a person who knows how to quest. You already know that the chaos outside can only be made whole by finding peace within yourself. The chaos creates pain and the pain creates questions. The questions lead to the search and the search itself is what transforms us into the ones who find the wonderful house of many levels. The house is the house where the soul is sovereign and the body is its organic, vibrant, living container. Here is where the many discoveries are made, and each seeker will be led to individualized tasks, one at a time.

What has taken eons as we humans have come to consciousness can now be accomplished relatively quickly once we understand the process. It can be quicker now because our memories have begun to return and we recognize, with a jolt of "quickening," when we have heard truth spoken and when something belongs to our knowing.

There is another, even more important factor in the speed at which we can now learn; it is that our hearts are being awakened. We have progressed through the awakening to consciousness of the root and the sexual chakras, through the opening of the power chakra, and now have finally come to the threshold where most of us are experiencing the wider opening of the heart chakra.* This is the point at which we can become more fully conscious and aware of who we are. No longer do we need

---

*Chakras—a word derived from Sanskrit meaning "wheel"—are points in the human body that are considered to be centers of life force (prana) or vital energy. It is commonly agreed that there are seven major chakras in the human body, from the root at the tailbone to the crown at the top of the head.

to be entrapped in the illusion of separateness, but can begin to really see the extension of ourselves in every part of creation. We have not yet discovered as a whole race what must be done to stop our collective suffering. But now we have both organs of intelligence to set to work on the problem: our brains and our very intelligent hearts. This is a massive step forward.

Soon we will realize that there must be many, many seekers willing to explore the chaos and darkness of the unconscious human condition. The way we do that is one at a time, by accepting that each of us holds a section of the unexplored "dark matter" inside. This work will be done mostly after our ascension to the Pleiadian realms. Again, we recall that this does not mean leaving the Earth planet, but rather raising her entire experience to a higher level of lived biological experience. There is where our next big task will be done with intelligence, compassion, light, and skill. We will find the skeins of chaotic, raw fibers waiting for us and weave it into glorious habitats for all.

As our hearts are right now being opened wider, we are changing. We are developing the capacity to work both inside and outside the limitations of form, remembering there is more to identity than the physical body reflected in the mirror. We now can perceive the immense mirror of the creation itself, and beyond even the physicality of that. We can choose to open our eyes and see the larger image of the "I" and realize that "I AM." We can realize that we are here in form because it is the plan that was conceived—immaculately conceived—in boundless love.

I speak as one sent ahead to tell you what I have witnessed.

You may believe me or not, but soon you will see for yourself that outside the boundaries and limitations of form there is still "I." Outside the laws of physics, biology, geology, and all the countless laws of "ologies" that govern the maintenance of physicality lie the treasure chests that hold the material for the second emanation of creation. The best has been saved for "next."

Shall I make it plainer if I try to say it this way? We are not just physicality; the greater part by far of our make-up is nonphysical and eternal. We hold the keys to that larger world within our biology. We are still evolving, and this is where the future leads us. We will learn to mine the inner resources in ways we have not yet realized are possible. We do not first have to die and pass into the realms that many of our companions have seen in near-death experiences. Those realms are within our biological grasp; we are hard-wired as living human beings to visit them and to work in them.

This is where I have come to live and this is where I invite you to come and see. Although I write in flowery prose that my heart prefers, I also see and know with my human intellect that these things are possible and are happening to enough of us that we may safely proclaim it as the next leap in evolution, coming to a theater near you—soon!

It is a tremendous task of both heart and will to dedicate our lives to this work of building Earth and to begin it while still in form. So many people are already living this dedication without even knowing how blessed they are and without knowing there is more help for them yet to come. Numerous others are still working with us from beyond the curtain that seems to separate us but cannot. I have met many of these wonderful beings, some still in human guise. But the true good news is that we have all we need to do the work now. The long-forgotten secrets are being remembered; the ancient sealed scriptures are being unlocked.

Planet Earth is the seedbed for the rose that already has fully blossomed in the pleroma, the fullness of divine vision. We have been living the experiences of childhood, even infancy, in our consciousness. In the same way that a child can understand the complexities of an adult's world, we have grasped our full potential.

We are spiritual beings having an experience in form, and as babies eventually learn what is for their own good, we, too, are learning. Children do and must think of their own interests first, but gradually they realize that sharing and compassion are also important to their own welfare. It takes much maturity to get to the point where the heart is fully open to the best interests of others.

Most children, at one time or another, strike out physically or verbally against a parent, even though they love that parent. Usually they are quickly repentant, for it bruises their own innocent hearts to do so. On this Earth where we are seeded and tended, we need modeling and guidance. Eventually we learn that to wound any one of us wounds us all. To malnourish any one leaf deforms the whole plant. The learning comes in very small baby steps here, and there is often great resistance because our hearts and eyes have not fully opened to see the principle of the One. Every one of us has been greedy and callous at some point, but we have patience with children and we are learning to have patience with ourselves as well.

However sophisticated, mature, or powerful we may feel ourselves to be, "Whoever would lead must serve the rest." That is the only true power there is; the rest is just the strutting of children trying on roles and testing their gifts.

It is time now for those who have more fully awakened to realize the next step of our growth. The word is used deliberately—real-ize—to make real the potential inside us.

We are at the turning point of an age and on the cusp of a huge step in evolution. For those who are ready—and you will know if you are—we are moving into the step called "ascension." Ascension happens as we fully open our hearts. The Pleiades is strongly related to Earth and is the first of the many mansions that have been prepared for us by the One who went before us to do so. The work of the beings there is to continue our ascension by teaching us more and more mysteries of the heart.

The heart is the organ of love, and Earth is and will be the organ of love in the cosmos. Pleiadians understand the deeper workings of the heart and are with us to shepherd us toward that sacred and deep knowing. You will understand that all of these words are metaphorical in the sense that we will not abandon our earthen jewel of a home, nor will the world end as we ascend. We are just learning to widen our consciousness and live on multiple levels simultaneously. We already live on multiple levels, but mostly have no awareness of it. Ascension means that we will have an awareness of the next level while staying grounded on Earth.

This is not something to be learned overnight; however,

the time will be shortened so that the human race can survive the shift. The more we cooperate with the many changes we will perceive with our senses and in extrasensory ways, the greater will be the ease with which we make the transition.

Over and over again, the Holy Mother has come to us and tried to prepare us for this time. In many places all over Earth she has come to teach us things to support this shift. One thing she has repeated several times is that the world is not ending, but we will experience the end of time. I may write more about that in the future, but here is what she basically means: we will learn to live in the present moment. History will no longer be what it is now. The only moment of importance will be the one we live in, one at a time. To do this we must allow all other moments to flow along—to give them up, to no longer carry them on our shoulders. We will learn true freedom as we surrender to the current moment.

As our hearts open—remember that this is the key—we are literally given access to previously unknown treasures. There is a built-in safeguard to the stores of material available to us. Without the fully opened heart, the courage we will find available to us and the motivation and ambition at new levels would be very dangerous and counterproductive. The knowledge and skills to use the materials available to us would be disastrous in the hands of competing children. As we grow up we learn about creative imagination and how to heal the wounds that have plagued and twisted our formation. We are given the means to hold a new image, untouched by biases and preconceptions, of an evolved, progressed, peaceful, and healthy Earth, and to bring it to life.

The creative material of the universe, still available since the stars burst forth from the void, is being put into our hands. This is what happens in the first heaven. We who have already ascended have seen for ourselves and are learning to work with what we have brought here from Earth through the Blue Spiral. Some of us are still living in bodies on Earth and others have passed on to higher levels while still keeping a presence here. We are given access to the greater plan for Earth insofar as we are capable of understanding it. We act as guides, mentors, architects, keepers, and in many other capacities to help those of you there to build the Earth. We sometimes call ourselves "Earth whisperers," a term we adapted from your language! We are here, we are real, we still care—even more so, we love you. Soon you will see as we do that we love the "us," the One, the All. It is an endless delight!

And this is only the first heaven. Just as we still enter into the adventures of the turquoise planet, others I am beginning to meet come to us here from higher worlds. There is no end to learning the blissful new information they bring. Perhaps one day I will be capable of writing about some of these higher planes, or perhaps there will be no need then, for an awakened heart can learn everything it needs and desires to know in its proper time.

THIRTEEN

Deeper into Mystery

If you have already entered the wonderful house in the Pleiades, you will be able to perceive the subtle differences between this and your former life's experience. First, the atmosphere is inviting, like a call to come further. Whether you are personally in sorrow or in joy, entertaining high hopes or struggling with dark distress, the burden is a little lighter. The walls feel sturdy with an abiding peace, and the passageways are redolent of deep expectancy. This is because you cannot enter here before you know you are loved no-matter-what and that the Holy One supports your every moment, in grief and in contentment.

There are countless ways to explore the mansion, but I will choose one, which you may prefer to follow just for this orientation tour. Remember, though, that when you and the house are ready, you will be drawn into its rooms in the order that is best for you. No one else can lead you then.

So we begin again with the tiny foyer. You are invited to remain alert to the living matter that forms its walls, floors, and odd-shaped openings. Inhale its living breath and know it is sentient and growing, transforming, just as you are. If you pay close attention, you can already catch the faint scent of the rose that it serves, still invisible at this moment.

We proceed to enter the breathtaking atrium on our left. If you have never entered here before, you will realize at once that it is sacred ground. We have all the time in the world, so pause and observe well. The Fountain of Living Water graces the center of the room with a pleasing, peaceful, preternatural bubbling forth of light and sound, reminiscent of ancient oceans and sweet springs of water in May. You will be surprised to realize that you are gazing, as if through the giant lens of the Hubble telescope, at the brink of creation itself, microseconds after the Word burst forth into form.

You see the thirteen women in a circle who receive these waters into their crystal goblets. Watch carefully as one of them holds her cup to be filled to the brim and offers it to you, the newcomer. Notice the chalice, which you perceive to be of pure diamond forged in the alchemy of the starry cosmos, reflecting the light until it dazzles the room with colors beyond human capacity to entertain. Reach out your hands willingly, lovingly, to receive the offering.

As you swallow the pure elixir of love you think of how little you have been aware of your own thirst until now and of how this water promises to never leave you thirsty again. Put your hands together, then, in a gesture of *namaste* and bow gently toward the presence who has thus greeted you.* You have received an amazing gift. As you withdraw from the

---

Namaste is a common Hindu greeting. Usually accompanied by a slight bow with hands pressed together, palms touching and fingers pointed upward, it means, "The God within me bows to the God within you."

chamber you are still stunned to have looked upon the cup that *is* the universe itself, in which you live and move and have your being, and to have been blessed to drink from it in your turn. You know now, at last, that it contains all you will ever need or desire. You silently thank the creature who has held it to your lips—your own soul.

Someday you may be invited to stand in that place as a cup-bearer and offer the water of life. When that day comes you may choose to accept the offer or not, for the cup is already yours as part of the All. You/we have created this Holy Atrium/Garden of the Cup for now, in order to learn the precious contents we hold and to offer it to other pilgrims. One day we may choose to manifest a different reality for those who will come. It is all a grand adventure into our deepest self.

When you are ready to resume the tour, we will continue on to the Hall of the Swords. You may have been tempted to think that these two sacred chambers represent a separation between women and men in this mansion. It is time to realize that each one of us, embodied or not, present on Earth as a woman or as a man, goes through both initiations, that of the cup and that of the sword.

In the Atrium you saw feminine aspects of all people who come to the awareness of being cup bearers. This is the feminine capacity in which they enter into the creative becoming of the universe. Through these feminine manifestations of the heart, the universe offers all it has and is to any traveler who asks for its precious gifts.

In the second chamber you will see the masculine aspects of all people who learn to take up the sword and awaken to its true responsibilities. You already know the profound dedication that this place represents. Let us now speak of the tremendous sacrifice this room honors in eternal witness. There is no awakening to the power of the sword without great sacrifice, for it demands discrimination. The sword is an instrument of discernment, above all else. It is an instrument of commitment, as well. The forging of the sword is done in the sacred fire that burns but does not consume. It is a lifetime's work, standing near and sometimes in the fire, crafting the instrument of your dedicated work in building the Earth.

The sword only takes its shape as each dedicated being allows the fire of the holy forge to burn away whatever is extraneous to the life to which we are called by love. This is a calling to stand for something worth keeping, worth loving, worth shaping. Sometimes it feels like a stripping and a purging, but these losses are building us into stronger steel to be ready to find the true riches of our shared life in the All. I speak not of some afterlife reward, but of abundance in the earthly plane on the many levels we discover as we become the strong and resilient instrument of our planetary emergence. As the sword grows huge and strong and eternal, so the masculine aspect of our being grows to meet and serve the challenges of life to be lived on the Earth planet; begun but not finished there.

While the feminine aspect in each of us is discovering the healing and relating wonders of the cup, the masculine aspect in each of us is discovering the active power of the sword as we forge it and then use it to protect the part of the garden we have been given to serve. This great hall is the place each of us has been or will be brought to make our consecration to the work of building the Earth and to the ongoing journey of the turquoise planet to fulfill its mission among the spheres, a journey we have not even begun to comprehend. Just as the women holding the cup are not usually aware, in their everyday life, of the sacred place they hold in the Pleiades, so the men forging the swords are not usually aware, in their everyday life, of the reason for the struggles and sacrifices asked of them. Nevertheless, both amazing processes are ongoing and are nurturing our becoming.

So, as each one completes the great work of crafting her/his weapon, it is placed here in the Great Hall. Out of sight of its maker, it eternally holds the fervor and dedication of the original commitment made by its forger, and it generates that power to that embodied being, enhancing the work being done wherever they are from then on. It does not deteriorate or lose its radiance. It is a thing that its maker can know and feel at times by faith alone, once it has been consciously crafted.

The sword and the cross are one, if one can receive this truth. The cross is the visual symbol of the earthen reality, with its polarities and seeming contradictions. The work of building the Earth involves coming to grips with these polarities and allowing them to resolve into something wonderful and new, beyond the current three dimensions. It will take a very high degree of spiritual awareness to finally resolve these contradictions without banishing them, but the Christ and others, who are all a part of that One Divine Presence, have already modeled the way. It only remains for us to understand what they have shown us. The fifth dimension, the way of "at-one-ment," is in the center of the cross, holding a place that does not move.

It is a still point where all the facets of the One can crystallize around it in all their diversity and uniqueness and be welcomed, celebrated, and held precious. The day will come, for we are being called higher. "Friend, come higher and receive the inheritance reserved for you from the foundation of the world!"

The sword is an image of that place that we shall deem the center and shall stand, unmoved, in it. When it is wedded to the feminine spirit of relatedness and receptivity, it can stand unmoved yet flexible. It is a paradox that can only be understood by one who has been forged in the fire and refreshed by the water. Have patience, for these things are not secrets to be kept, but experiences that can and will be learned.

Pause, if you will, and closely examine the immense weapons hanging here. Is one of them yours? Have you already crafted it and need only to believe in it? Or does that experience lie ahead for you? If and when you are led to this room on your own quest, do not falter, but put everything you have into the effort, for it is the way to the future of Earth and all her related journeys. God give you wings for your feet and for your heart to come here and join in the great forging of the future!

If you are ready to come into the library, I will show you around. But please know that this room requires a lot from you. If you return here later, it will be because you have been invited, and it will mean a wonderful, intensive, dedicated chapter in your life, whether you come here while embodied or in another form. Let me explain.

I hope you will be heartened, if you feel drawn to enter here, by the fact that many, many of us have been able to do the task of this place while still embodied and while continuing to manage other tasks and relationships in our lives. It is fascinating work and very fulfilling, as much as it is demanding. As with everything, if you feel the call to do it, it will be bliss and you will be graced to do it. You will also, at times, wonder why you ever decided to come here. Which of our many choices is ever not like that?

As we enter the lovely library of this mansion, we will probably first notice the pictures hanging on all the walls. There is an important message coded in the images there, as you will discover when you have spent enough time here. These images are really memories that have been gathered, honored, and pondered by the entire lineage of our humanity. An event is not over in the way we think that history takes place and is over. The event becomes an image, inscribed in the cells of our physicality and the workings of our psychology, as well as in our spirituality. It becomes a thing of myth, at times gaining numinosity as it expands in our consciousness. People, places, and things become something more as the event blends with our imaginative faculties. This is because we are chemical beings as well as electrical and gravitational beings. Life on Earth is a constant swirling together of sense input, DNA molecules, chemistry, and what we think of as fantasy.

We are building the Earth according to the way all crystals grow. Each new bit of reality crystallizes around something that is already there. This is the pattern of earthen life. If we search for the patterns, we will find them, despite the many ways they are hidden in the warp and woof of the personal experience. We will look for patterns in the images and will discover the marvelous process of co-creation.

Images are the key component of what we are building. All of the messages and guidance we need to evolve further are in us. The pattern for the new heavens and new Earth is already there. Truth and beauty, a new physicality, a subtler form of matter, are crystallizing slowly around the patterns within us.

The immortality of history is not about "who" did "what" and "when," because there is only now and only we. The real gift of history is about origins, ideals, and roots, cultural beliefs and the patterns that lie beneath the many-colored fabrics of the stories.

> *For whenever the powers of the soul make contact, they set to work and make an image and likeness of the creature, which they absorb. That is how they know the creature. No creature can come closer to the soul than this, and the soul never approaches a creature without having first voluntarily taken an image of it into herself.*
> MEISTER ECKHART (C. 1260–1328 CE)

In a way that is almost totally inexpressible, the soul is learning what it is like to have a body, to be human, to feel emotion. It delights in these experiences and is helping us to learn (for that is why we have been "sent") and capture these experiences. They are being woven into a more subtle form of materiality that can be "assumed into heaven." Everything that is genuine of our earthen experience will be present in a richer form as we co-create the new Earth, the fulfillment of the garden.

So I am reminded, over and over again, to honor and cherish my humanity, body and soul, corporeal and spiritual, and bring the subtle essence of this creature whose life I now live with me as I ascend. I will, in doing this, bring all humanity with me in the Christ (or in whatever name you choose to call this Holy One who has and will come) back to the Source. I will have done what Mary, the Holy Mother, has done, and I can only do it because she has done it and opened the way for us. I will also, as Jesus did, prepare a place for you who cannot follow immediately, and I can only do that because he first prepared a place for me.

For ages, it seems, humans have wished for someone who has passed through the veil to the other side to tell them what they have found there. It is important that you realize this book is not being channeled by someone on the other side, but is being written from firsthand experience by someone who is alive now and has ascended to the next level.* It is written with permission from the Holy One to speak now so that you may be able to follow, if you are ready. It may be that these words are just planting seeds in your heart and mind that will come to fruition in their time and help you then. It doesn't matter which way it happens, for some will hear now and follow and others later, all in their perfect time. Having passed through the portal of the opened heart, I live now on Earth, but I'm constantly in touch with the fifth dimension. This is where we are all going.

---

*Channeling is the process of receiving messages or inspiration from spiritual beings or entities, often said to be intended for others, that are usually passed on either verbally or in writing.

Why is it that certain images of people or gods or hero/ines capture our imagination and grow larger than life and more inspirational as we gaze at them? We are already looking at the reality of the "who" that we are, but we have not yet been able to recognize the divinity within ourselves. But the grandeur and splendor is already there, living in us, loving us, helping our dense, mortal components to grow into the possibility for recognition. As we continue to honor the images we love and which inspire us, they are drawing more of the same to us, as the crystal draws more of its like material to it. The new world is crystallizing around the core we are building through these images. Even though we do this process alone, we add greatly to the dynamic new world coming into existence right now. The truth is that each of us must do it alone, regardless of whether others are working with us toward this goal, for everything depends on the individual effort.

The building material for creation is always chaos. When we have chaos, we have ample material for shaping order and beauty. The creation myths of all cultures tell us one or another version of the world coming forth from some form of chaos. Today we have almost enough chaos to build anything we wish if we can but realize our divine Source. We are being coaxed and prodded awake to arise to our glorious heritage.

How shall we best work with what we have already? The divine seed falls into the soil of Earth to materialize. Earth is the seedbed for the rose, as was said earlier. But each individual seed falls into the soil that is best for its individual growth. It falls into a culture, a nationality, a society that is faith-based or not, a family, and a global family as well. It is important that each one develop into a unique representation of divinity on this Mother Planet. Diversity is what will make the new creation strong, healthy, vibrant, and interesting. The combination of spirit (divinity) and matter (physicality) is a marriage that bears the true Messiah, if you will. The promised One of ages is what is gestating in us, both challenged and assisted by the growing chaos.

Study your own culture's images, those of your faith, of your hero/ine tales. Nurture the images in your own heart and collect new ones as they call to you. Learn who you yourself are in your uniqueness by allowing patterns and connecting threads to merge and synthesize within you as they catch hold of your creative imagination. See if you can trace continuity for yourself and your clan, as people have done since before recorded history, by listening to and reading the stories. Find patterns that reveal the macrocosm hiding in the microcosm.

Ask for guidance from advanced beings who have walked Earth's pathways before you and have been guided to the wonderful secret truths. They can help you to learn who you are in the eternal sense and give you a much broader view from which to watch your temporal body and mind growing and searching. You can learn to be the observer as well as the observed. Sketch or paint from your imagination, caring not one whit for how it looks, but only for what it stirs in your soul. Sketch and paint until you have found your own truth and can hang it on the walls here in the Pleiades. Or compose your own songs, poetry, or music in the same manner—for your ears only until your soul responds and sings back to you a song to hear in eternity.

We are learning new ways entirely, ways that are really as old as time. Practice the new until we all begin to see the desert bloom and the new creation rising out of the chaotic void.

In the midst of all of this meaningful and important work of building the Earth, you will discover the secret of the merkabah—the amazing chair that is the flying chariot to take you to other realities. As I said, I cannot lead you there. Only your own diligent and devoted work will reveal it to you. It is a secret of empowerment that is veiled from those who would use it for their own gain or frivolous purposes. But those whose hearts are centered on the One will be led to every tool and assist needed. You don't enter this library until and unless you have decided to dedicate yourself to the work, in whatever way is your own.

Are you ready now to revisit the Gathering Room? We passed through it very quickly on the first visit. Now we must look a little more carefully into what happens there. To understand better, it may be helpful to speak again of the Immaculate Conception, which is the Divine Plan for Earth, if understood properly. Recall that this is a name that belongs to all materiality, not to the Catholic Church or any other organization. It does not even belong exclusively to the Mother of Jesus, if you can understand this. She is the icon of the title, the image that was intended to quicken our consciousness of what the created world is in God's eyes. It matters not one bit what your name for God is or what faith you may follow; this is a metaphor. Please do not mistake it for a doctrine of a particular religion, or you may not be able to follow the truth concealed and revealed in it.

The Immaculate Conception is a view of created (physical) reality that reveals the way God so loves and cherishes it. In the way that Mary of Nazareth was able to conceive Jesus because she had a physical body, so Earth herself is conceiving and gestating a divine birth through the bodies that live, grow, and die here. Earth (matter) is the beloved partner of spirit, as was declared before all time. As Mary is declared the Mother of God, the entire Earth is truly bringing forth the body of God in a much more cosmic way, but one that follows the pattern that Jesus and Mary actually lived.

We have largely completed our childhood relationship with the universe. We have now entered into the age of real partnership with one another and with God. It only remains for us to accept and live this enormous privilege and power. It is time for our ascension to the next level of conscious participation in the work of building and maintaining Earth and nurturing the gestating divinity among us. In truth, this infant child is quickening and is already a miraculous, living presence among us. It is this inner divine self that is now informing and directing our future growth. The Christ returns within—in glory!

I believe that a great sign of this cosmic quickening of the gestating Divine Child is one that was given on Christmas Day, 2012, in the little village of Medugorje, Croatia, where the Gospa (her name for herself), or Our Lady of Medugorje, has been appearing since June of 1981. This hamlet of vineyards and pomegranates is bursting with the symbolism of the vineyard parables we have heard in scripture. The Lady of the Vineyard has come there to remain as a presence overseeing these years of the great in-gathering, years of tuning in to the quiet inner guidance that will save our world from the path it seemed doomed to follow. She is supervising the evolutionary shift we are experiencing that is raising the consciousness of Earth to a point of ascension. We will begin to live our own nature and use our own gifts for the good of all. For many years she has been giving monthly messages of hope and inspiration to one or another of the original group of six visionaries to whom she first appeared.

Her words have come to me in all those years, as well, as one who cannot be separated from the rest. Several of my dear friends have received her messages, too. It is through her teaching and intimacy in prayer that I have come to learn the things I bring to you now, so imagine the delight I felt when I heard the message given that December in Medugorje to Marija, who received these words. At this appearance, the Mother carried her baby with her—the Divine Child. For the first time it was he who delivered the message. The Divine Infant spoke! If you have the ears to hear, it means that the child now has a voice to speak. The brand-new infant of God's marriage with humanity now has a voice. It is as if to say the "still, small voice" of God, heard by Elijah in the Book of Kings, is ready to speak wisdom to all. The actual words spoken were simple, but profound: "I AM your peace."

It is now the grand turning point at which we can accept or reject the partnership. To do this we are not required to accept any new doctrine other than that of the Law of Love. We are called to the awesome task of loving the planet, our fellow beings, and ourselves in a new and more pervasive way.

Our hearts now will reveal the intelligence and power they hold, kept sealed until we were mature and loving enough to be trusted with such power. This opening of the heart, in all people everywhere, is a truly grand event in the cosmic scheme for all the worlds.

As our love matures and deepens, more knowledge will seep into our minds because there are treasured secrets that the heart alone knows. Knowledge without love is dangerous! As our hearts open, courage floods into us, because we begin to know that speaking truth is the surest way to our deepest power, evolution, and understanding of the treasures we hold as a diverse creation.

Courage without love is dangerous. As our love, knowledge, and courage mature and we begin to join our efforts without thinking first of personal gain, great power will flow in and among us.

Power without love is dangerous. We will finally see power we could not dream of while we held to our personal greed and ego desires. The desires of the ascended self have no enjoyment from the pain or disadvantage of others, for this is no longer even an accepted notion of our knowing ourselves. We reach the great "Aha!" of our oneness and desire nothing so much as unity in our diversity. We are delighted to enhance the "other," for we see how it enhances our own true happiness.

What will it mean to have all the valid knowledge and information that has been gathered by all the individuals, all the species, all the flora, fauna, and mineral elements of Earth's whole experience at the disposal of each one of us as we need it? For a time, when my little "I" was still in the density of the Earth's gravity, I believed it would be fantastically absurd to think that we could experience omniscience or anything near it. But here in the first heaven I grasp the significance of that term. It is not a matter of any one individual having such a vast storehouse of knowledge available at all times. It is a matter of each of us contributing to that storehouse to the extent we are able and, in the ascended body, being able to reach into the storehouse at any moment and know what is necessary right then. As I move along my path and open my heart to the impulses from my brain as well, I am being shown and given everything in every moment that is necessary for my own task.

The problems over which we now strain and groan all have answers here on this other level, where we have joined ourselves and learned from one another. Where we refuse to see our connections or honor them, there are blockages in the grid of information. Humility, trust, and willingness to learn dissolve the blockages and allow the communication without words, keeping vital information flowing along the dendrite-like connections that surround and envelop us all. Soon we will need fewer words, have fewer language barriers, and experience fewer delays in communication.

If we close our hearts, it is to our own detriment.

After that slight digression, please join me in the Gathering Room. Are you beginning to see what we are gathering in this room, here in the Pleiades? Remember that this is not a place like Washington, New Jersey, or even the Sea of Tranquility on the moon. It is a metaphorical place in the collective psyche that we all share. Some may have called it the Akashic

Records in the past. Père Teilhard de Chardin,* the inspired scientist and mystic, called it the "noosphere" in 1922 in his *Cosmogenesis*. He presented this gathering as a new planetary sphere that joins the hydrosphere, the atmosphere, and all the many spheres that support life on the planet. We are supported by these in common; no one owns them. The noosphere contains the collected wisdom of all forms of life on the planet, but especially human consciousness—the consciousness of Gaia, the one organism that we collectively are. I still prefer to say the consciousness of the Immaculate Conception that could only be held by matter, in God's beloved, who "ponders all things in her heart" (Luke 2:51).

So here we are again, in the Gathering Room. And what does this room ask of you, if not to willingly place your unique life experience—your knowing and loving, what wounds and what heals, what engenders growth and what hinders it—at the disposal of the One?

The unique experience of yours is something that the One can know in no other way. The great and mighty ones of the planet may think they can discover answers that nurture it, but life is designed in such a way that no one person and no group can know what is truly needed for life to flourish.

---

*Teilhard de Chardin (1881–1955), a French Jesuit priest who trained as a paleontologist and geologist, conceived the idea of the "omega point," the highest level of complexity and consciousness the universe could achieve, and popularized the concept of the noosphere. He wrote two comprehensive works: *The Phenomenon of Man* describes the unfolding of the cosmos and the evolution of matter through humanity to an ultimate reunion with God in the Cosmic Christ. *The Divine Milieu* supports the Jesuit belief that secular work—including scientific work—is an integral element of incarnation; that human efforts are transformed in the "divine milieu."

We do not need to write articles and letters to give our input. This is the exoteric (outer way) of sharing wisdom. It is good in its place, but woefully inadequate for the tasks ahead. The surest, safest, and most effective way of inputting your wisdom and experience is directly into the All. This is the meaning of assumption, just as Mary was assumed into heaven. The gathering task is the way we teach divinity what it is like to exist in biology. We each have different experiences, and divinity wants and needs to know all of them. Your needs are no less than the needs of kings, queens, saints, and beggars. Your truth is no less true or important than that of scholars and sages, street-smart folk and the mentally challenged.

When you have done the work of sorting and gathering your own wisdom, then it is time to turn it over to the All. When you are hurting or wounded, it is time to hand over those feelings to the All to be registered in the great diary or journal of Earth's life. All the celebratory moments, as well as all the traumatic ones, need to be recorded there in order for the total needs of the planet to be known and met.

When you are ready, devotedly place yourself, just as you are in your moment in time, into the center of the Blue Spiral. Do it alone or with others whom you trust. It is a sacred trust—being a record-keeper for the great experiment of our descent into form. We are researching for the future to know how biology can better support the great weight of divine glory.

You will not do this once and for all. Once you have consciously been initiated into this ceremony, you will do it many times a day, in just a flash of intention. It is part of your assumption into heaven.

Although the term "assumption" has been used in connection with the dogma of the Blessed Mother, meditation reveals the meaning, which is that the human body is the delight of the Divine, who draws it into the sacred marriage chamber to be One forever. Once you have begun to understand you will see that we, who are spiritual beings, have descended to Earth for the purpose of experiencing biological life and of bringing that experience of a body back with us when we ascend.

The body we bring along is not the dense, clay container it started out to be. It has been shaped and nurtured, loosened up by the chemical reactions it undergoes in the earthen seedbed. It is grown from that soil, but upon entry here is no longer purely clay. It is interpenetrated by the many elements on Earth that have exchanged molecules with it as it grows into the perfect rose or lotus, both of which represent the flowering of consciousness. It has also been interpenetrated and inseminated with spirit, whose light falls equally on all.

We slowly ascend without seeing how and what and when, and we bring with us the essence of the beautiful, marvelous turquoise planet of love. We do not leave Earth; it ascends into its rightful place in the cosmos.

For this purpose we see, in this present work, an imperfect image of this truth as it is happening. Over and over again the Sacred Mother has taught and urged me to accentuate the great dogma of her Assumption. More than any other concept, it needs to be understood right now. Great faiths the world over have taught much about other facets of our visit to Earth, but this concept has been misunderstood and overlooked. I have not read it in any other source. It is the work of the Blue Spiral, our connection to the higher worlds. It is the way that more advanced beings work together with earthlings to support and bring forth the gift that Earth has to offer to the entire cosmos.

It is still the early morning of universal life, but as it dawns with all its radiance, Earth will be a gem from the royal depths, polished and set as a circlet or diadem to be worn by the All. We cannot yet imagine the glory of this dawning. As a lover says to the beloved in the *Song of Songs,* "Set me as a seal upon your heart and upon your arm," we will offer ourselves to the cosmos, for Earth will be where the heart first blossomed forth with the white rose of love.

I think of the gorgeous diamond—the Heart of the Ocean—that linked the lovers and all who knew them in the film *Titanic.* Our stone/rose/planet will be called the Heart of the Universe. We will be and already are the planet of love, where feeling and true remembrance can flower into dimensions of love we have not yet seen. We do not have to wait until an afterlife to encounter it; it is right here among us as soon as we decide to open to it.

As book 1 Corinthians tells us, all things will pass away, even the virtues of hope and faith, but love remains always. We of Earth will someday lead others, beings from beyond our current knowing, into the ways of love. This is where they will come to learn what we are just beginning to craft and shape into our future blessing.

You are invited into the house—into the "first mansion" of many—where we will craft the Earth anew. Give up anything you must to follow!

PARTICLES AND WAVES

I like what your

        waves

              are doing to my

      par ti cles

dancing atoms   shiver

    as your coursing rays disturb them—oh!

      so sweetly—

dust motes in the   sunlight

    each curving

          wave

             enfolds

my every speck of matter . . .

        making love at the brink

                of creation,

you and I, holy Light,

    blending two, once again, into bliss.

MARY T. BEBEN

Background image by Steveroche.

BOOKS OF RELATED INTEREST

The Pleiadian Agenda
A New Cosmology for the Age of Light
by Barbara Hand Clow

Awakening the Planetary Mind
Beyond the Trauma of the Past to a New Era of Creativity
by Barbara Hand Clow

Bringers of the Dawn
Teachings from the Pleiadians
by Barbara Marciniak

Family of Light
Pleiadian Tales and Lessons in Living
by Barbara Marciniak

The Pleiadian Workbook
Awakening Your Divine Ka
by Amorah Quan Yin

The Council of Light
Divine Transmissions for
Manifesting the Deepest Desires of the Soul
by Danielle Rama Hoffman

Planetary Healing
Spirit Medicine for Global Transformation
by Nicki Scully and Mark Hallert

Shamanic Breathwork
Journeying beyond the Limits of the Self
by Linda Star Wolf

INNER TRADITIONS • BEAR & COMPANY
P.O. Box 388
Rochester, VT 05767
1-800-246-8648
www.InnerTraditions.com

Or contact your local bookseller